An Economic Value of Remote-Sensing Information—Application to Agricultural Production and Maintaining Groundwater Quality

By William M. Forney, Ronald P. Raunikar, Richard L. Bernknopf, and Shruti K. Mishra

Professional Paper 1796

U.S. Department of the Interior
U.S. Geological Survey

U.S. Department of the Interior
KEN SALAZAR, Secretary

U.S. Geological Survey
Marcia K. McNutt, Director

U.S. Geological Survey, Reston, Virginia: 2012

For an overview of USGS information products, including maps, imagery, and publications,
visit http://www.usgs.gov/pubprod

For more information on the USGS—the Federal source for science about the Earth,
its natural and living resources, natural hazards, and the environment, visit
http://www.usgs.gov or call 1-888-ASK-USGS (1-888-275-8747).

To order this and other USGS information products, visit http://store.usgs.gov

Suggested citation:
Forney, W.M., Raunikar, R.P., Bernknopf, R.L., and Mishra, S.K., 2012, An economic value of remote-sensing information—Application to agricultural production and maintaining groundwater quality: U.S. Geological Survey Professional Paper 1796, 60 p.

Contents

Abstract 1

Introduction 1

    Background 2

Conceptual Framework and Economic Model 3

    Value of Information Theory 5

Empirical Application and Methods 6

    Agricultural Production 7

    Nitrate Contamination of Aquifers 7

        Dynamic Nitrate Pollution 10

            Capture-Zone Delineation 12

            Crop-Area Calculation Using MRLI 13

            Nitrogen-Leaching Estimation 13

        Hazard Function and Groundwater Survival 15

    Value of Information Estimation 18

        Without MRLI Case 18

        With MRLI Case: Enhanced Landscape Configuration 18

Materials and Data 19

    Northeastern Iowa Study Region 21

    MRLI: Cropland Data Layer 21

    Crop Price Data 24

    Wells 25

    Hydrogeologic Characteristics 26

    Soil Characteristics 28

    Slope, Depressions, and Topographic Position 28

    Rivers, Watersheds, and Hydrologic Response Units 30

Results and Discussion 30

    Agricultural Production 30

    Nitrate Contamination of Aquifers 30

        Dynamic Nitrate Pollution 30

        Leachate Estimation 32

        Groundwater Vulnerability 37

    Value of Information Results 39

    Additional Discussion 43

    Future Research 43

Summary and Conclusions 47

Acknowledgments 47

References Cited 48

Appendixes 54

    Appendix 1—Integrated Assessment Approach's Assumptions and Their Types 55

    Appendix 2—Nitrogen Cycle 56

    Appendix 3—Kriging of Hydraulic Conductivity 57

Figures

1. Diagram showing conceptual framework for the integrated assessment approach. Adapted from Antle and Just (1991) 4
2. Diagram showing production possibilities frontiers (PPF) for crop production and the survivability of potable groundwater 6
3. Diagram showing conceptual factors of the decisionmakers' framework across space and time for the empirical application of the integrated assessment approach 8
4. Diagram showing conceptual schematic for models and biophysical drivers of the empirical application of the integrated assessment approach. 9
5. Graph showing trends in corn and soybeans in the 35-county northeastern Iowa study region, 2001–2010 10
6. Diagram showing the nitrogen cycle 11
7. Map showing ArcAEM/Split model output and capture zone result on the National Agricultural Statistics Service's 2007 Cropland Data Layer...14
8. Map showing watersheds, rivers, and digital elevation model for the study region in northeastern Iowa. These geospatial datasets are also used as ArcSWAT inputs 15
9. Diagram illustrating arbitrarily interval-censored data used for the proportional hazards model 18
10. Map showing case study location in reference to the full extent of National Agricultural Statistics Service's 2007 Cropland Data Layer for the Midwest 20
11. Map showing the distribution of capture zones (CZs) delineated using ArcAEM/Split for the northeastern Iowa study area, which includes 35 counties 22
12. Map showing crop rotation patterns with the National Agricultural Statistics Service's 2007 Cropland Data Layer in a small part of the northeastern Iowa study region, which includes the City of Waterloo, 2000–2010..23
13. Graph showing average annual real prices received for corn grain and soybeans by U.S. producers. The data are derived from the monthly Agricultural Prices reports of the National Agricultural Statistics Service, Agricultural Statistics Board, U.S. Department of Agriculture...25
14. Map of Iowa showing a sample of National Water quality Assessment Program (NAWQA) wells in Silurian, Devonian, and Ordovician aquifers and cities in the northeastern Iowa study region 26
15. Map showing interpolated well depths for the 35-county northeastern Iowa study region. ..27
16. Map showing derived Silurian and Devonian aquifer thicknesses in the northeastern Iowa study region. Source is Iowa Department of Natural Resources. 28
17. Map showing shaded relief of topography for the 35-county northeastern Iowa study region...29
18. Subbasin-level yield maps for combined corn and soybean production estimated from ArcSWAT for the northeastern Iowa study region, 2001 to 2010..33
19. Maps showing subbasin-level nitrate leaching associated with corn and soybean production estimated from ArcSWAT for the northeastern Iowa study region, 2001 to 2010. Avg., average; kg, kilograms..38
20. Graph showing groundwater-survival probability curves of three subbasins in the 35-county northeastern Iowa study region 39
21. Map showing groundwater failure and subbasin probability of survival for the northeastern Iowa study region..40
22. Bar graph showing annual flow of benefits with and without moderate-resolution land imagery (MRLI) for the 35-county northeastern Iowa study region 41

23. Map showing the net present value estimates for the value of information (VOI) calculations at the subbasin-level that overlap the 35-counties in the northeastern Iowa study region 42

24. Image of regression kriging without residuals, using hydraulic conductivity for the 35-county northeastern Iowa study region as an example 58

25. Image of kriging regression residuals, using hydraulic conductivity for the 35-county northeastern Iowa study region as an example 59

26. Image of final regression kriged layer, using hydraulic conductivity for the 35-county northeastern Iowa study region as an example 60

Tables

1. Description of data used for estimation of economic value of remote-sensing information in the northeastern Iowa study region 17

2. Shifting imaging sensors, accuracies, and metrics of the National Agricultural Statistics Service's Cropland Data Layer, 2000–2010..24

3. Crop yield estimates and area calculations for four land-use/land-cover (LULC) types of the northeastern Iowa study region, 2001–2010 31

4. Summary statistics for cumulative nitrate indicator (CNI) data 34

5. Ordinary-least-square estimates for cumulative nitrate indicator equations. 35

6. Arrelano-bond dynamic panel-data estimation results for cumulative nitrate indicator equations 35

7. Arrelano-Bond dynamic panel-data estimations using three categories of thickness for Quaternary deposits..36

8. Average nitrate leaching rates and total leached amount estimated from ArcSWAT for the northeastern Iowa study region, 2001–2010 37

9. Proportional hazards model estimated effects of explanatory factors on probablitly of well survival (equation 20) 37

10. United States corn and soybean production estimates and projections, 2000 to 2026, from Food and Agricultural Policy Research Institue (2012)..44

11. Natural Resources Conservation Service (NRCS) land conservation programs summary for the 35-county northeastern Iowa study region, 2003 to 2011 45

12. United States biofuels production and feedstock source estimates and projections, 2005 to 2025, from Food and Agricultural Policy Research Institue (2012)..46

13. Log-log regression equation for kriging of hydraulic conductivity in Devonian and Silurian aquifers in the northeastern Iowa study region..57

Acronyms and Abbreviations

AEM	Analytic element method
ArcGIS®	ESRI™ geographic information systems software
ArcSWAT	Soil and Water Assessment Tool for use with ArcGIS
AWiFS	Advance Wide Field Sensor
CDL	Cropland Data Layer
CNI	Cumulative nitrate indicator
CLU	Common Land Unit
CPI-U	Consumer price index for all urban consumers
CZ	Capture zone
DEM	Digital elevation model
DSS	Decision support system
EAI	Equivalent annual income
EPA	Environmental Protection Agency
FAPRI	Food and Agricultural Policy Research Institute
GMM	Generalized method of moments
HC	Hydraulic conductivity
HRU	Hydrologic response unit
HUC	Hydrologic unit code
IAA	Integrated assessment approach
IDNR	Iowa Department of Natural Resources
JAS	June Agricultural Survey
LCDM	Landsat Data Continuity Mission
L/min.	Liters per minute
LULC	Land use/land cover
MCL	Maximum Contamination Level
mpd	Meters per day
MODIS	Moderate-resolution Imaging Spectroradiometer
MRLI	Moderate-resolution land imagery
NASS	National Agricultural Statistics Service
NAWQA	National Water Quality Assessment Program
N_2	Nitrogen gas
NH_3	Ammonia
N_2O	Nitrous oxide
NO_3^-	Nitrate
NHD	National Hydrography Dataset
NPV	Net present value
NRCS	Natural Resources Conservation Service

OK	Ordinary kriging
OLS	Ordinary least squares
PPF	Production possibility frontier
RATS	Estima, Inc., Regression Analysis of Time Series software
RFS	Renewable Fuel Standard
RK	Regression kriging
STATA	StataCorp LP statistical software
USDA	U.S. Department of Agriculture
USGS	U.S. Geological Survey
VOI	Value of information
WGSC	Western Geographic Science Center

This page intentionally left blank.

An Economic Value of Remote-Sensing Information— Application to Agricultural Production and Maintaining Groundwater Quality

By William M. Forney[1], Ronald P. Raunikar[1], Richard L. Bernknopf[2], and Shruti K. Mishra[3]

Abstract

Does remote-sensing information provide economic benefits to society, and can a value be assigned to those benefits? Can resource management and policy decisions be better informed by coupling past and present Earth observations with groundwater nitrate measurements? Using an integrated assessment approach, the U.S. Geological Survey (USGS) applied an established conceptual framework to answer these questions, as well as to estimate the value of information (VOI) for remote-sensing imagery. The approach uses moderate-resolution land-imagery (MRLI) data from the Landsat and Advanced Wide Field Sensor satellites that has been classified by the National Agricultural Statistics Service into the Cropland Data Layer (CDL). Within the constraint of the U.S. Environmental Protection Agency's public health threshold for potable groundwater resources, the USGS modeled the relation between a population of the CDL's land uses and dynamic nitrate (NO_3^-) contamination of aquifers in a case study region in northeastern Iowa. Employing various multiscaled, multitemporal geospatial datasets with MRLI to maximize the value of agricultural production, the approach develops and uses multiple environmental science models to address dynamic nitrogen loading and transport at specified distances from specific sites (wells) and at landscape scales (for example, across 35 counties and two aquifers). In addition to the ecosystem service of potable groundwater, this effort focuses on the use of MRLI for the management of the major land uses in the study region—the production of corn and soybeans, which can impact groundwater quality. Derived methods and results include (1) economic and dynamic nitrate-pollution models, (2) probabilities of the survival of groundwater, and (3) a VOI for remote sensing. For the northeastern Iowa study region, the marginal benefit of the MRLI VOI (in 2010 dollars) is $858 million ± $197 million annualized, which corresponds to a net present value of $38.1 billion ± $8.8 billion for that flow of benefits in perpetuity. Given that these economic estimates are derived from one case study in a part of only one State, the estimates provide a lower estimate related to the potential value of the Landsat Data Continuity Mission.

Introduction

This study demonstrates the value of information (VOI) of moderate-resolution land imagery (MRLI)—which mostly includes Landsat imagery—using a case study of agricultural production and preservation of groundwater resources in the agricultural State of Iowa. The MRLI is used widely in several sectors; however, the societal value of the operational application of the scientific information provided by MRLI has not been quantified. In the analysis here, we use an integrated assessment approach (IAA) in the context of public health to estimate the value of MRLI. Our research has concentrated on documenting changes in two ecosystem services and the economic tradeoffs and impacts of those changes. Systematically, the analysis links spatiotemporal Earth observations to the maintenance of a certain level of groundwater quality over time, while maximizing the value of production on agricultural land. By linking the Landsat data archive to a groundwater vulnerability model, a probabilistic forecast can be made of when, where, and how long an aquifer system would retain its potability. This report comprehensively evaluates the coupling of archival Earth observation imagery and land uses to hydrogeologic and ecosystem-science process models, demonstrating an economic benefit and a positive value of scientific information in agricultural and natural-resource decisions.

The intent of the case study is to demonstrate the use of remote-sensing imagery to assist in natural-resource management of corn and soybean crops in 35 counties in eastern Iowa. MRLI can assist with identifying suitable places for types of agricultural production that may require nitrogen fertilizer, which can contaminate groundwater. Over a 10-year period of analysis, we found that some groundwater wells are threatened

---

[1]U.S. Geological Survey.

[2]University of New Mexico, Albuquerque, New Mexico.

[3]U.S. Geological Survey contractor.

by nitrate (NO_3^-) contamination and could fail to maintain drinking-water quality in the next 10 years and that other locations where the topography, soils, well characteristics (such as depth and operations), and surficial geology are less likely to transport the contaminant to the water supply in the future. Given that VOI estimates require an application in which the information in question is used, the case study has created a suite of integrated models that can be used as a decision support system (DSS) by interested stakeholders. For example, a regulator could decide whether to intervene to impose a reduction in fertilizer application or change the distribution of crop-production patterns to reduce the probability of a public or private well failure.

This case study shows that a new application of MRLI potentially provides significant societal benefits from Landsat imagery. It is likely that many new applications of MRLI have the potential to become important additions to the enhanced management of land use/land cover (LULC).

Background

Currently, a question faces Congress and the Nation as to allocating and maintaining the resources necessary to a particular MRLI sensor, namely Landsat. As part of the Landsat Data Continuity Mission (LDCM) to maintain the series of satellites first launched in 1972, the launch of Landsat-8 is planned for February 2013. The output of Landsat is information and the U.S. Geological Survey (USGS) policy was established to provide minimally processed Landsat imagery at zero price (Landsat Science Team, 2008). The policy defines the information as a public good because a market for the information does not exist. As with any ambitious, high-cost endeavor, interested stakeholders will want to know, "Is it worth it?" A way to answer that question is to quantify the benefit of having the information available to public-sector decisionmaking versus a situation where it is not, which is one definition of VOI (Bernknopf and others, 1997; Macauley, 2005). The analysis here is an input to the justification of the continuation of the Landsat mission as a public good that requires a quantitative economic approach and development of a method to estimate the societal benefits of providing the information. The MRLI and its classified derivatives provide a spatiotemporal LULC signal that can be used for making decisions in preservation and management of resources. This research estimates the economic VOI for a particular usage of MRLI.

This research estimates the VOI of MRLI using an IAA to assess the impacts of environmental pollution based on farm activities in the agricultural sector of Iowa. The VOI is estimated as (1) the economic benefit stream of a net increase in agricultural production across a region without sacrificing groundwater resources and (2) how the characterization and management of agricultural production and its environmental impacts may change with or without the availability of MRLI. The analysis is an examination of the nitrate accumulation

patterns in wells of Iowa. Benefits of MRLI accrue to society by avoiding the risk of exceeding the nitrate water-quality standard in groundwater as a result of efficient changes in land-use patterns. A second objective of the research examines the capability of MRLI to inform the management of agricultural production for the benefit of individual producers, as well as for the benefit of societal welfare. The widespread and diffuse nature of nonpoint source contamination of groundwater from crop and livestock production makes the determination of sources and opportunities for control and remediation very difficult (Rodvang and Simpkins, 2001). Thus, the ability to utilize MRLI to observe regional scale LULC and use it as an input into the characterization of its impact on natural resources across a region is appealing. Over time, the archive of Earth observation of land-use patterns can be used to monitor and document how producers' decisions can affect ecosystem services in socially relevant and policy-relevant contexts.

A number of social welfare considerations, policy drivers, and other factors helped to define the orientation of this research on this particular case study. First, applications in environmental science and management (40 percent), LULC (17 percent), planning and development (11 percent), and the agricultural sector (8 percent) have been documented as the four largest application areas of Landsat for all user sectors (Miller and others, 2011). In addition, Miller and others (2011) continued to identify agriculture and environmental science in the Federal sector as the largest application areas. Second, biofuel production from corn ethanol and other sources was incentivized by the Energy Policy Act of 2005, which set the Renewable Fuel Standard (RFS) to increase ethanol levels from 4.0 to 7.5 billion gallons per year by 2012. The Energy Independence and Security Act of 2007 increased those RFS levels to require the use of at least 36 billion gallons of biofuel by 2022—15 billion gallons being corn ethanol and the remainder being cellulosic ethanol (such as perennial grasses, biomass, and municipal solid waste) and other advanced biofuels. Third, the increase in renewable fuel production could not occur independent of constraining public health policies such as the Federal Clean Water Act of 1972 and Safe Drinking Water Act of 1974, State water-quality codes, Groundwater Protection Acts, and manure management plans. Most importantly for this work, the U.S. Environmental Protection Agency (EPA) established the threshold Maximum Contamination Level (MCL)[4] of 10 milligrams per liter (mg/L) nitrate (measured as nitrogen) for safe drinking water. Finally, the U.S. Department of Agriculture's (USDA) and Natural Resources Conservation Service (NRCS) conservation programs (for example, Crop Reserve Program, Wetland Reserve Program, Environmental Quality Incentives Program) provide economic incentives in the form of voluntary, yet binding, cost-share programs to farmers to take their lands out of

---

[4]EPA list of contaminants and their Maximum Contaminant Levels: http://www.epa.gov/safewater/contaminants/index.html.

production, which exacerbates the complexity of understanding changes in LULC and agricultural production.

Drinking water exceeding the MCL of nitrate causes human health impacts such as methemoglobinemia, which in infants is also known as "blue baby syndrome." Nolan and Hitt (2006) documented that adverse health impacts such as miscarriages and cancer risks were noted in populations with drinking water with nitrate levels higher than 2.46 mg/L. Nitrate is not a carcinogenic compound; however, it reacts with other chemicals to form carcinogenic compounds, such as nitrosamines and nitrosamides that are associated with multiple different types of cancers (Mirvish, 1995; Weyer and others, 2001; Ward and others, 2005). In addition, Mirvish (1995) stated that disruption of thyroid function, birth defects, and hypertension are other results of ingesting nitrate. It is also important to note that some countries such as Germany and South Africa have a much stricter standard for drinking-water nitrate levels set at 4.4 mg/L (Kross, 2002).

Conceptual Framework and Economic Model

The primary components of the conceptual framework (fig. 1) include decisions at the levels of the individual farmer and regulators both with and without spatiotemporal MRLI information and how MRLI data relates to agricultural production, environmental pollution, and the joint production of agricultural products (corn and soybeans) and groundwater contaminants (nitrates) in a landscape (Bernknopf and others, 2012). Adapting an IAA from Antle and Just (1991), our IAA illustrates how MRLI can inform production and regulatory decisions. The decisions by individual producers in the site-specific production of the joint output of a marketable agricultural commodity (Antle and McGuckin, 1993) and a nonmarket service of groundwater quality are reflected in figure 1 (boxes 1 through 6). The decisions by public agencies and other stakeholders involve regional-scale land-use decisions and their impact on ecosystem services (fig. 1, boxes 7 and 8). The MRLI observations of regional crop production and rotation when linked to the current level and future accumulation of nitrates in the groundwater, and the environmental risks associated with historical, current, and possible land uses, provides value by informing potential reallocation of regional land use in order to preserve ecosystem services associated with groundwater resources. The VOI is estimated for MRLI using equation 1 to maximize agricultural production for any given location within the region, while avoiding an increase in groundwater pollution from those agricultural nitrogen sources.

The regional model incorporates both the producers' (an individual's or microeconomic perspective) and the regulators' (a regional or macroeconomic perspective) priorities in accommodating the overall decisionmaking process. The regional economic model is based on an individual producer's objective to maximize profit, while constraining risks of a marketable crop in equation 1 (fig. 1, boxes 1–6). Given a vector of regulations $\mathbf{R}$, producers seek to maximize profit on each plot of land:

$$\max_{\mathbf{q}_t,\mathbf{v}_t,\mathbf{z}_t} \sum_{t=t_0}^{\infty} d^t \pi(\mathbf{q}_t,\mathbf{v}_t,\mathbf{z}_t,\mathbf{P}(\mathbf{R})_t,\mathbf{W}(\mathbf{R})_t,\mathbf{e}_t), \quad (1)$$

$$s.t. \quad \mathbf{e}_{t+1}=\mathbf{e}_z+\Delta\mathbf{e}(\mathbf{q}_t,\mathbf{v}_t,\mathbf{z}_t)$$

$$\mathbf{R}_t^{q\min} \leq \mathbf{q}_t \leq \mathbf{R}_t^{q\max}$$

$$\mathbf{R}_t^{v\min} \leq \mathbf{v}_t \leq \mathbf{R}_t^{v\max}$$

$$\mathbf{R}_t^{z\min} \leq \mathbf{z}_t \leq \mathbf{R}_t^{z\max}$$

$$F(\mathbf{q},\mathbf{v},\mathbf{z},\mathbf{e};\mathbf{R}) \geq 0$$

where $\mathbf{P}$ represents prices of relevant crops and crop production ($\mathbf{q}$) is the amount of each crop produced on a plot of land and is a function of variable inputs ($\mathbf{v}$), farm management practices ($\mathbf{z}$), and plot characteristics ($\mathbf{e}$). Discounting is by factor d, π is the annual profit function for farmers in the region, $\mathbf{W}$ is input costs vector, and $\mathbf{R}$ is explicitly shown as minimum and maximum regulatory constraints (*s.t.*) on the decision variables and subsidies applied to the prices and costs the producer faces. (Note that in equations in this report, italic represents a scalar and bold represents a vector.) Current choice variables affect the future by the changes they cause to the physical properties of the plot by the function. Time, t, is discrete corresponding to planting decisions made each annual growing season. Planting decisions are based, in part, on past prices that form expectations for a new crop in the upcoming year. In terms of aggregating the estimation of joint output and conducting statistical analyses for regional policy analysis, we assume an annual basis is appropriate.

Moving from the individual producer to the regional perspective, our study region is a limited fraction of world soybean and corn production so that marginal changes in production do not have a significant effect of crop prices, $\mathbf{P}$. Thus, the partial equilibrium approximation of policies $\mathbf{R}$ not affecting $\mathbf{P}$ is appropriate. Note that $\mathbf{Q}$ (aggregate, regional production of crops) and $\mathbf{P}$ are vectors of quantity and present discounted real price of corn and soybeans for each year of the analysis. Therefore, $\mathbf{PQ}$ is the present discounted value of the corn/soybean crop over that time period and subject to the regional risks. The regional production model in equation 2 represents activities associated with regulator choices (fig. 1). Like individual producer decisions, in the aggregation of joint output and conducting statistical analyses for regional (macroeconomic) policy analysis, we assume an annual basis is appropriate. Regulatory standards originate as regional decisions based on scientific analysis of the human health effects of specific agrochemical usage. We approximate the regulator's problem as:

$$\max_{\mathbf{R}} \mathbf{PQ}$$

$$s.t. \ \mathbf{risks} \leq \boldsymbol{\alpha} \quad , \quad (2)$$

Both the plot level and regional risks are related to the quality of information about crop production, variable inputs, farm management practices, plot characteristics, and α, which represents the probability of exceeding regulatory standards that cause damage to a natural resource (groundwater).

A societal choice involves decisions at the regional scale and has an overarching effect on a variety of individual landowners and firms. As stated above, EPA has established the national standard for the regulation of nitrate contamination at 10 mg/L, which can be applied regionally and locally to protect the public supply of drinking water. The regulator solves equation 2 acting as if α is given, but this acceptable risk is also the result of an optimization process (a risk standard is assumed

to be the result of scientific trials) at the higher level of authority of the policymaker. The expected present discounted value of the policies to society, especially local residents and their aggregated improvement in public welfare, can be optimized by choosing a particular $\mathbf{R}^*$ from possible policies Γ:

$$\max_{\mathbf{R} \in \Gamma} \pi^s (\mathbf{R}, \alpha(\mathbf{R})) \cdot \tag{3}$$

The choices of policymakers reveal social preferences.[5] We can infer α^* from observed regulatory outcomes. This inferred α^* is the risk constraint to which regulators have

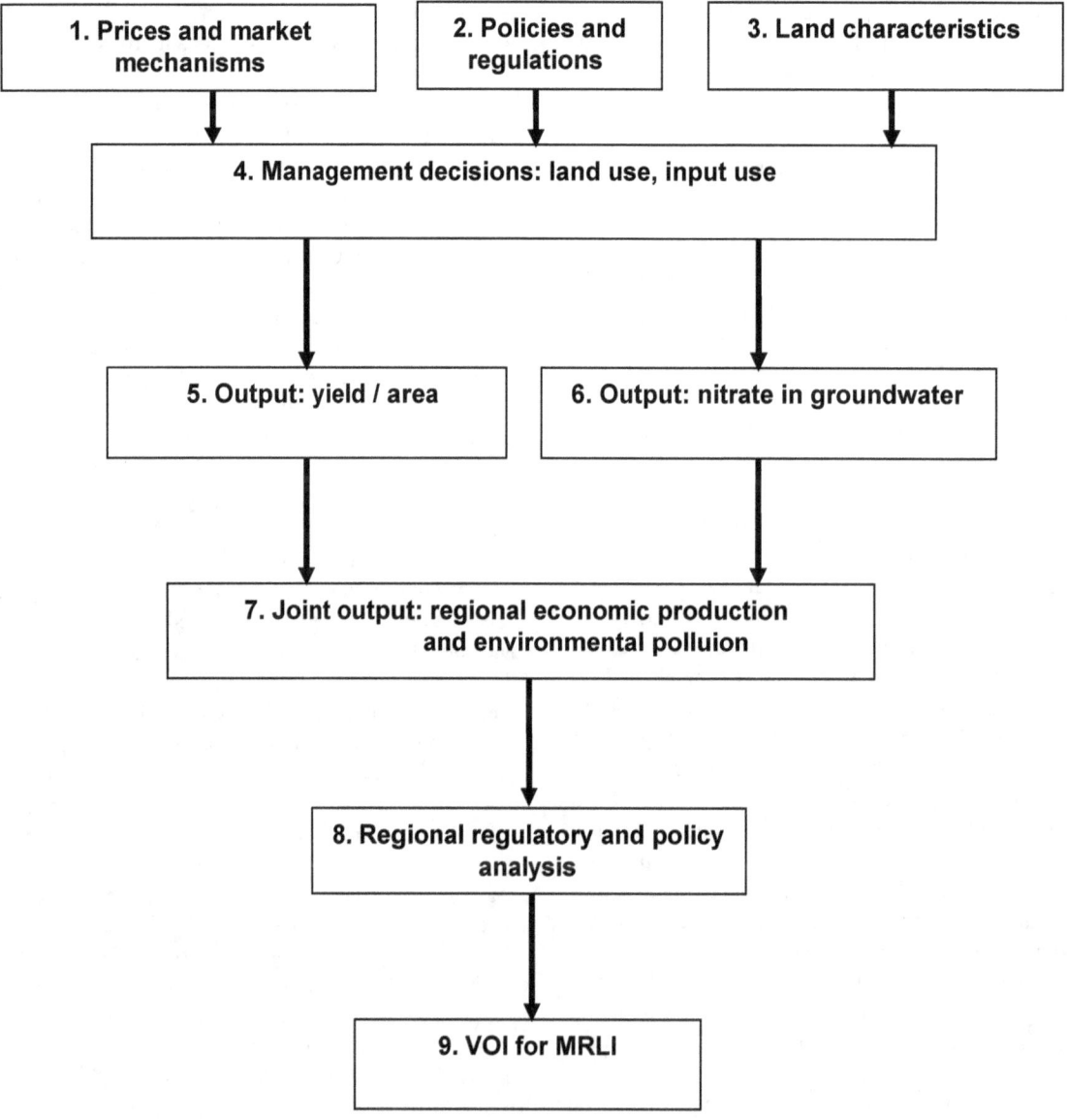

Figure 1. Diagram showing conceptual framework for the integrated assessment approach. Adapted from Antle and Just (1991). VOI, value of information; MRLI, moderate-resolution land imagery.

conformed, and we assume it is a reasonable risk constraint for the future to apply to marginal alterations of policy or to the case of improved information structure. Over long periods of time, production of corn—and to a lesser degree the production of soybeans—its associated pollution, and its cumulative environmental effects at regional scale can cause substantial changes to groundwater. The policy issue is whether the ecosystem service of potable groundwater becomes stressed and could be compromised, or even lost, because of changes in the land-use pattern, location, and intensity.

The regional economic model has a number of assumptions that make the agricultural application more tractable for empirical demonstration. Appendix 1 lists the model assumptions for individual producers, regional-scale output, and the other models and analysis of the IAA.

Value of Information Theory

The final calculation in the IAA (fig. 1, box 9) is the estimation of the economic value of the MRLI. In estimating a dollar value of the Earth observation information, it is assumed that the regional market is competitive and is operating efficiently. Because the requirements for a functioning competitive economy are achieved, the joint output of the economy for a production scenario is a point on the regional production possibility frontier (PPF) in figure 2. Using equation 3, different estimates of efficient outcomes of the joint output of crop production and the survivability of potable groundwater can be plotted along the PPF for each set of policies, **R**, in a LULC scenario.

The MRLI input is a unique technological innovation that when applied to improve on a current land-use allocation, creates an outward shift in the PPF from PPF_0 to PPF_1 (Buckwell, 1989; Mas-Colell and others, 1995; Varian, 1999); that is, society could have a more valuable mix of agricultural production and greater survivability of potable groundwater. The VOI for the MRLI is derived from this outward shift in the PPF. In figure 2, points A and B on PPF_0 are two efficient allocations of land for crop production and the survivability of potable groundwater. Point A represents a regional economy that has a high level of crop output and low survivability of potable groundwater. Point A maximizes crop production given a particular level of surviving, potable groundwater. Point A could be current and historical crop patterns as shown by the Landsat archive. Alternatively, point B represents a regional output that lowers the risk of losing potable groundwater by accepting a crop production of lower value as a tradeoff. Point B could be a highly regulated amount of crop production to sustain a large quantity of high-quality groundwater and could be considered a

conservation alternative. Points A and B are alternative optimal solutions of regional land allocation without MRLI. Point C on PPF_1 improves the regional allocation of land with MRLI by taking advantage of the technological advances in Earth observation. Point C indicates that a reallocation of land use would increase both crop production and retain the existing survivability of potable groundwater. Point C is a reallocation of land use based on the linkage between MRLI observation and classification of agricultural products and physical-process models of groundwater vulnerability to identify better locations for particular land uses.

Using equation 4, we estimate the value of **P**Δ**Q** for the application of estimating the benefits of MRLI. The existing regulations with the additional information from MRLI ($\omega(1)$) would be $\mathbf{R}^*(\omega(1),\alpha)$ and without additional information ($\omega(0)$) would be $\mathbf{R}^*(\omega(0),\alpha)$ for the probability of exceeding the regulatory standard for resource damage, α. The additional information may allow regulations to be better targeted so that the crop production will be different $\mathbf{Q}^*_{\mathbf{R}(\omega(1),\alpha)}$ with the information (at point C on PPF_1 in fig. 2) than without $\mathbf{Q}^*_{\mathbf{R}(\omega(0),\alpha)}$ (at either point A or point B on PPF_0 in fig. 2). Therefore, the VOI to the regulator is stated explicitly as:

$$VOI_{\omega(1)} = \mathbf{P}\left[\mathbf{Q}^*_{\mathbf{R}(\omega(1),\alpha)} - \mathbf{Q}^*_{\mathbf{R}(\omega(0),\alpha)}\right]. \qquad (4)$$

The present discounted value, **PQ**, for the range of years analyzed is calculated by summing the quantities of corn and soybeans produced in each land unit into the time series **Q** and multiplying by the present discounted vector of real prices that prevailed during the period of analysis. A possible combination of cropping choices across the study region is eliminated if the environmental constraint is exceeded, and among those choices not eliminated, the optimization algorithm steps through cropping choices until a maximum **PQ** is identified and annualized. The present discounted value of the difference between optimal (with MRLI and associated modeling data) and baseline (without MRLI data) is **P**Δ**Q**. The VOI expressed as an equivalent annual income (*EAI*) is:

$$EAI = \mathbf{P}\Delta\mathbf{Q}\frac{r\,(1+r)^t}{(1+r)^t - 1}, \qquad (5)$$

where *r* is the discount rate. Assuming a similar flow of benefits into the indefinite future because of the continuation of the availability of MRLI, for this region the net present value (*NPV*) is calculated:

$$NPV = EAI\frac{(1+r)}{r}. \qquad (6)$$

This net present value is an estimate of the value of using MRLI based information for managing the corn/soybean crop patterns and groundwater resources in our study region into the indefinite future.

---

[5]Others have used observed government actions to reveal social preferences. McFadden (1975) inferred the revealed value of indirect costs and benefits to highway route selectors, and Ross (1984) shows how revealed preference can be applied to infer the implied social-weighted sum of preferences of regulators. We are not using revealed preference to infer values, but rather to infer the optimal constraints implied by those values.

Empirical Application and Methods

This section focuses on discussing the technical aspects necessary to apply empirically the conceptual framework (fig. 1) and the methods derived for achieving that application in the case study region of northeastern Iowa. The application requires the consideration of the more germane driving factors of individual producers and government regulators (fig. 3). Along the continuum of space from smallest to largest, a field includes farm-management practices and land characteristics, a farm includes crop rotation patterns and the influence of lands in the USDA's or NRCS's conservation programs, a county is the level to which agricultural statistics are reported and the without MRLI VOI base case is estimated, a region is susceptible to distribution of climate (temperature and precipitation), and the State and Federal governments dictate overriding energy and regulatory policies. Along the temporal continuum from shortest to longest, commodity prices and weather can vary in a given week; farm management practices, regulatory policies, and accumulation of pollution can occur or be imposed over months and seasons; crop rotations and

changes to LULC vary over seasons to a given year; the estimates of joint output occur on an annual basis; and a particular site's land characteristics, the changes to energy policies and the duration of USDA and NRCS conservation program contracts are on the order of 5 to 10 years (although some land characteristics like soil texture can change more quickly from farm-management practices and some conservation program contracts such as those of the Wetland Reserve Program[6] contain permanent easements). These scales influence the spatio-temporal units of analyses for the research.

In this research, the primary units of analyses include fields, counties, wells, capture zones (CZ), hydrologic response units, watersheds and aquifers. The empirical application is summarized in a schematic (fig. 4), which presents the joint output agricultural products and groundwater contamination, land-use transitions, leachate from the soil, surface areas that represent CZs for particular wells, accumulation of nitrate in a well in a time-dependent indicator, and an aquifer's likelihood of survival

---

[6]For more information on the Wetland Reserve Program see http://www.fs.fed.us/spf/coop/programs/loa/wrp.shtml.

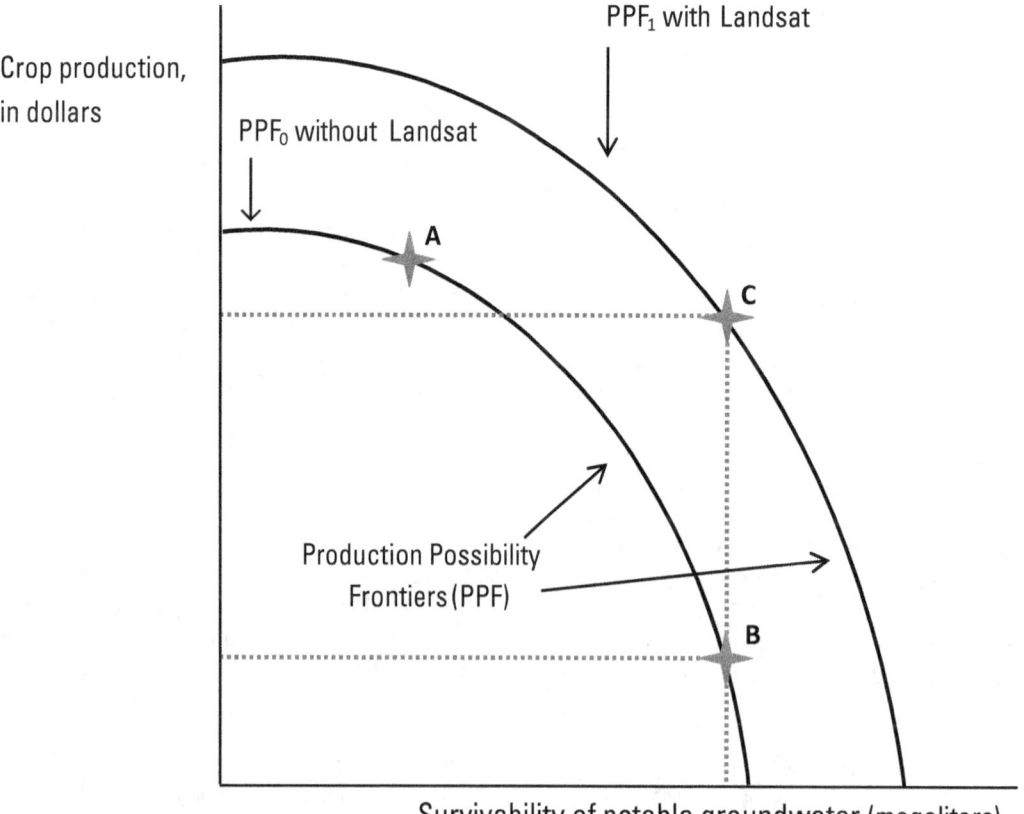

Figure 2. Diagram showing production possibility frontiers (PPF) for crop production and the survivability of potable groundwater.

in the long run. The empirical aspects of the research are further described in the following sections on agricultural production, nitrate contamination of aquifers, and estimation of VOI.

Agricultural Production

Crop production is a function of variable inputs (**v**), farm management practices (**z**), and plot characteristics (**e**) (eq. 6 in Bernknopf and others, 2012). Previous studies estimated crop production and fertilizer using a quadratic function, such as the von Leibig and Mitscherlich-Baule functions (Frank and others, 1990), apply agricultural production and yield data at the county level (Farajalla and others, 1993; Liao and others, 2012), and have used annual tonnage of nitrogenous fertilizer shipped into a county as a proxy for direct measurement of application rates (Farajalla and others, 1993). This research in this report relies on the capability of remote sensing to classify agricultural production by crop type at a field-scale resolution and then to develop site-specific, model-based estimates of crop production and fertilizer application rates.

The largest percentage of Iowa's farmland (76 percent) is devoted to croplands, with 92 percent of these crops dedicated to corn and soybeans (Causarano and others, 2008). The Cropland Data Layer (CDL) from the National Agricultural Statistics Service (NASS) provides estimates of land in corn and soybean production from 2001 to 2010, which shows a general trend toward increasing corn production and decreasing soybean production (fig. 5). Because of their significance in ethanol production and typical crop rotation patterns, the particular crops of interest are corn and soybeans. We considered fractionation of the types of corn into such commodities as grain, food, and silage; however, the LULC system we used did not provide such a distinction, and we assumed that the difference in nitrogenous fertilizer application and its resulting effects on groundwater quality would be minimal.

Corn and soybean yields were estimated with an Arc-GIS® version of the Soil and Water Assessment Tool (Arc-SWAT) (Neitsch and others, 2009). ArcSWAT is a physically based, nonpoint source model and was developed to estimate crop yields and predict impacts of land management on water, sediment, and agricultural chemical yields in complex, large watersheds with differing soils, land uses, and climate and landscape characteristics. ArcSWAT has been applied widely.[7] In an improvement over the simplifications of previous economic models of crop production, ArcSWAT's plant growth model is based on inhibition by temperature, water, nitrogen and phosphorous availability, accumulated heat units, the Monteith potential biomass method, and a harvest index to calculate yield.[8] ArcSWAT categorizes plants into seven different types and varies their treatment on such factors as nitrogen fixation

simulation, growth of roots, and dormancy. The seven types are (1) warm season annual legumes, (2) cold season annual legumes, (3) perennial legumes, (4) warm season annuals, (5) cold season annuals, (6) perennials, and (7) trees. As is suggested by Bock and Hergert (1991), Kapp (1986), and Bourg (1984), the model matches fertilizer application rate to the needs of the crops and climatic conditions by timing it with the accumulated heat index. Including a drying time needed for harvesting dry weight, the yield of a particular crop is defined as:

$$yld = bio \times \left(1 - \frac{1}{(1+HI)}\right) , \qquad (7)$$

$$HI = HI_{opt} \times \frac{100 \times fr_{PHU}}{(100 \times fr_{PHU} + exp\,[11.1 - 10 \times fr_{PHU}])} , \quad (8)$$

where, *yld* is the dry-weight crop yield in kilograms per hectare (kg/ha), *bio* is the harvested aboveground biomass, *HI* is the potential harvest index for a given day, HI_{opt} is the potential harvest index for a particular plant at maturity and with ideal growing conditions, and fr_{PHU} is the fraction of potential heat units accumulated throughout the growing season. Yield is estimated by ArcSWAT at the hydrologic response unit (HRU) level, of which there are a number for any given watershed or subbasin.

Nitrate Contamination of Aquifers

Nitrate pollution in groundwater resources is a type of stock pollution, or a pollution that accumulates over time. Depending on the environmental characteristics of the groundwater system, there may be little capacity for the system to absorb additional nitrates. Nitrate loading from sources such as fertilizer, sewage, atmospheric deposition, and manure that leaches through the vadose zone, is transported through stratigraphic layers, and can accumulate in and contaminate aquifers over the years. Nitrate accumulation dynamics in groundwater is determined by nitrogenous compounds activities in the soil surface (for example, fertilizer and other nitrogen sources, land-use and management practices, properties of soil, and precipitation), movement of nitrate to aquifers (subsurface geology and age and recharge of the groundwater system), and denitrification of accumulated nitrate in aquifers. The following paragraphs describe the science, context, approach, and methods of nitrogen sources, fate, and transport in our research.

Figure 4 provides a conceptual schematic of the fate and transport of nitrate, as well as of the germane processes of groundwater contamination in this study. If the nitrogen source is an agricultural field, shallow and deep infiltration and transport of nitrate are observed in private wells (typically shallower) and municipal wells (typically deeper). The influx of uncontaminated groundwater from outside of the boundary condition of the case study region can dilute the concentration of nitrate. The two-dimensional (2D) surface

---

[7]For a sample of applications, please see http://swatmodel.tamu.edu/applications/.

[8]This harvest index is expected to be relatively stable across a range of environmental conditions.

represents the possible presence of an aquitard. The nitrogen deposited into the soil surface undergoes one or more of the processes of nitrogen cycle, depending on various physical, chemical, and biological properties (fig. 6 and appendix 2). The degree of leached-nitrate attenuation as the contaminant moves through the subsurface depends on the stratigraphic layers through which it passes (as represented by brown ovals in fig. 6), the time it takes to do so, and the distance the pollutant has to travel through unsaturated materials in the vadose zone to reach groundwater. In the unsaturated zone, the processes dictating fate and transport include infiltration, evapotranspiration, dilution, filtration, sorption, ion exchange, biochemical transformations and plant uptake, and volatilization. These processes are influenced by soil texture, permeability, temperature, thickness, pH, organic matter content, exchange capability, and acid neutralizing capacity. Some of these processes and

characteristics also influence the degree of nitrate attenuation in the saturated zone. In the entire hydrogeologic system (in other words, unsaturated and saturated zones), additional factors related to vulnerability include net recharge from irrigation and (or) precipitation, depth to the water table, and the gradients of flow (Canter, 1997; Committee on Techniques for Assessing Groundwater Vulnerability, 1993).

Earlier studies on groundwater nitrate pollution are primarily oriented toward static groundwater pollution models. Tesoriero (1997), Rupert (1998), and Eckhardt and Stackleberg (1995) estimated the probability of exceeding particular groundwater nitrate levels using well depth, groundwater recharge, soil hydrologic group, soil drainage, surficial geology type, land-use type, and population density. Nolan and others (2002) used a logistic regression to estimate aquifer susceptibility to nitrate pollution as a function of fertilizer

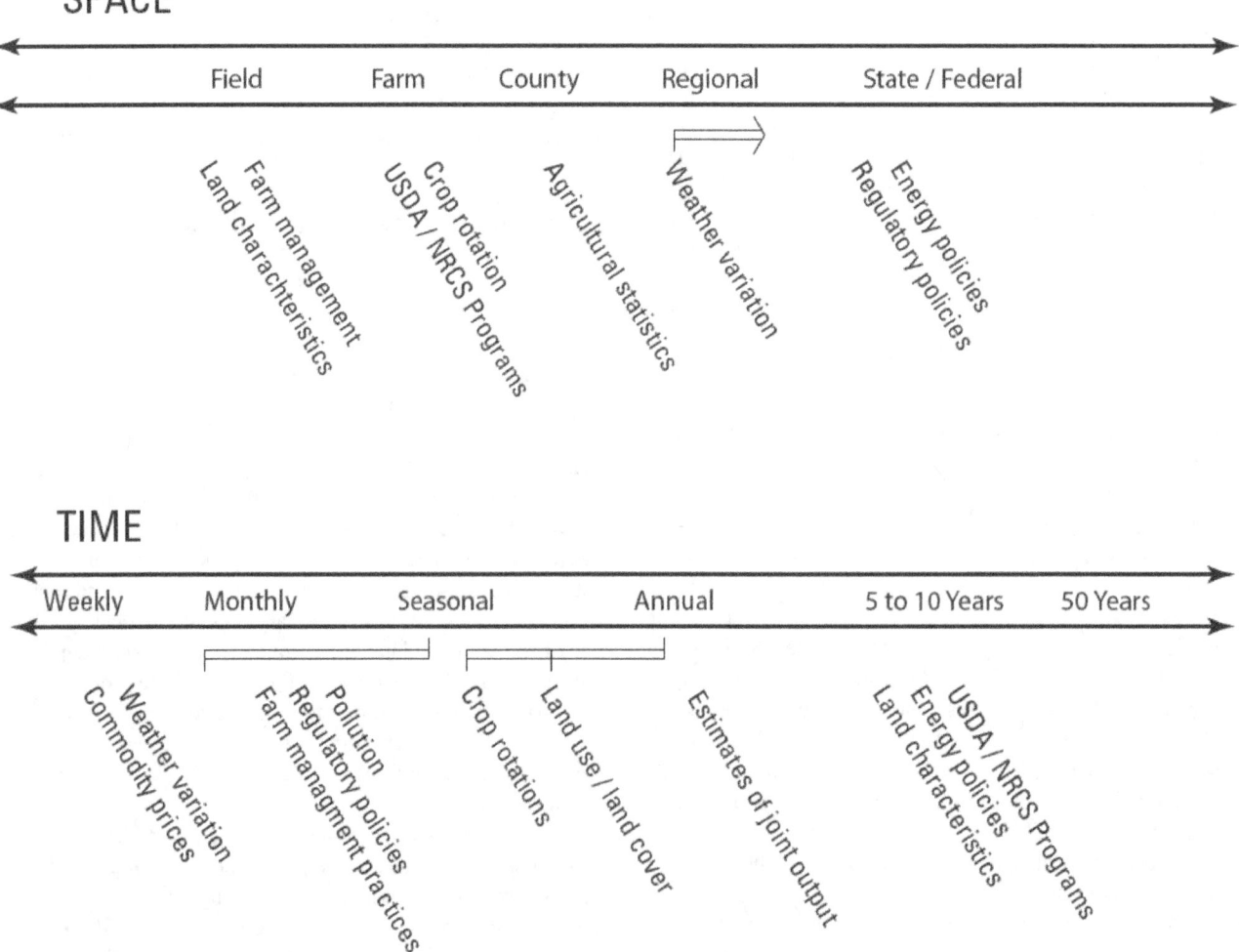

Figure 3. Diagram showing conceptual factors of the decisionmakers' framework across space and time for the empirical application of the integrated assessment approach. The bars, tick marks, and arrow under the time and space axes represent the range of scales and intervals, respectively, to which the conceptual factors apply. USDA, U.S. Department of Agriculture; NRCS, Natural Resources Conservation Service.

nitrogen loading, percent cropland-pasture, human population density, percent well-drained soils, depth to the water table, and presence or absence of a fracture zone within an aquifer.

Other research on groundwater nitrate pollution focused on estimating nitrate concentration in wells instead of probability of pollution. Litchenberg and Shapiro (1997) estimated nitrate concentration in Maryland Community Water System wells as a function of hydrological conditions for well and vector of land-use activities in recharge zone of the well. A comprehensive study by Nolan and Hitt (2006) estimated groundwater nitrate concentration in shallow and deep aquifers as a function of different nitrogen sources, nitrate transportation factors, and attenuation factors using nonlinear regressions. They estimated nitrate concentrations separately for shallow and deep wells, as deeper wells are likely to have better groundwater quality and different driving factors related to that better quality. For the shallow wells, nitrogen source variables are farm fertilizer, manure from confined animal feeding operations, orchards/

vineyards, population density, croplands/pasture/fallow; transport is explained by water input, carbonate rocks, basalt and volcanic rocks, drainage ditch, slope, glacial till, and clay; and attenuation is explained by fresh surface water withdrawal, irrigation tailwater recovery, histosol soil type, and wetlands. For the deep wells, nitrogen source variables are farm fertilizer, manure from confined animal feeding operations, orchards/vineyards, population density; variables explaining transport to aquifer are water input, glacial till, semiconsolidated sand aquifers, sandstone and carbonate rocks, drainage ditch, and Hortonian overland flow; and attenuation is explained by fresh surface-water withdrawal, irrigation tailwater recovery, dunne overland flow and well depth. These models do not explicitly consider the dynamic, temporal nature of the groundwater pollution problem associated with shifts in land-use patterns and repeated application of fertilizers; however, they do provide insights for modeling groundwater nitrate dynamics to reflect the changes in nitrate over time associated with changing land use.

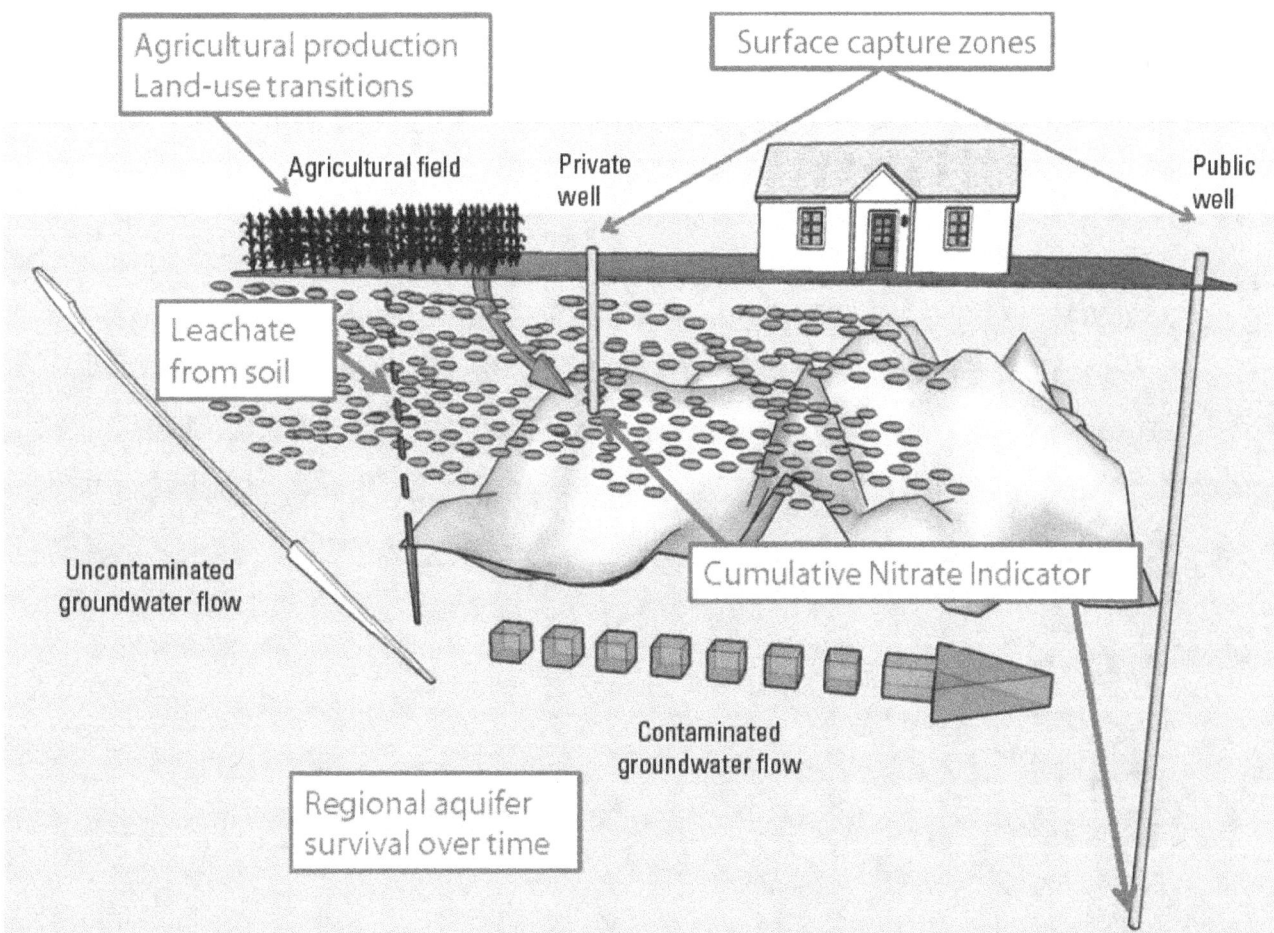

Figure 4. Diagram showing conceptual schematic for models and biophysical drivers of the empirical application of the integrated assessment approach.

Another important factor to consider in the mechanism of groundwater vulnerability is the degree to which an aquifer at depth is connected to land-surface processes. One factor can be described as confined versus unconfined groundwater systems (Prior and others, 2003). Confined groundwater systems are more protected by aquitards that have minimal pore space, high presence of sedimentary rocks and colloids, and minimal presence of preferential flow paths that can result in lower levels of nitrate contamination (Rodvang and Simpkins, 2001; Tesoriero and Voss, 1997; Nolan and others, 1997; Mueller and others, 1995; and Kross and others, 1990). Unconfined aquifers can have highly fractured bedrock and conduits for preferential flows of rapid groundwater infiltration and solute mobility via advection (Rodvang and

Simpkins, 2001; McKay and others, 1993), which are often present in limestone and dolomite bedrock formations.

Dynamic Nitrate Pollution

In this research, the accumulated nitrate pollution that has moved through the hydrogeologic system and, observed over time in a given well, is modeled as a difference equation (Yadav, 1997; Kim and others, 1993), referred to as the cumulative nitrate indicator (*CNI*). The *CNI* uses the measured nitrate level in the current and previous time periods and the addition of nitrate to the existing pool or amount in the given year from the nitrogenous fertilizer applied over the defined period of time. The difference equation estimates the annual change or the dynamics of nitrate concentration over the given time period.

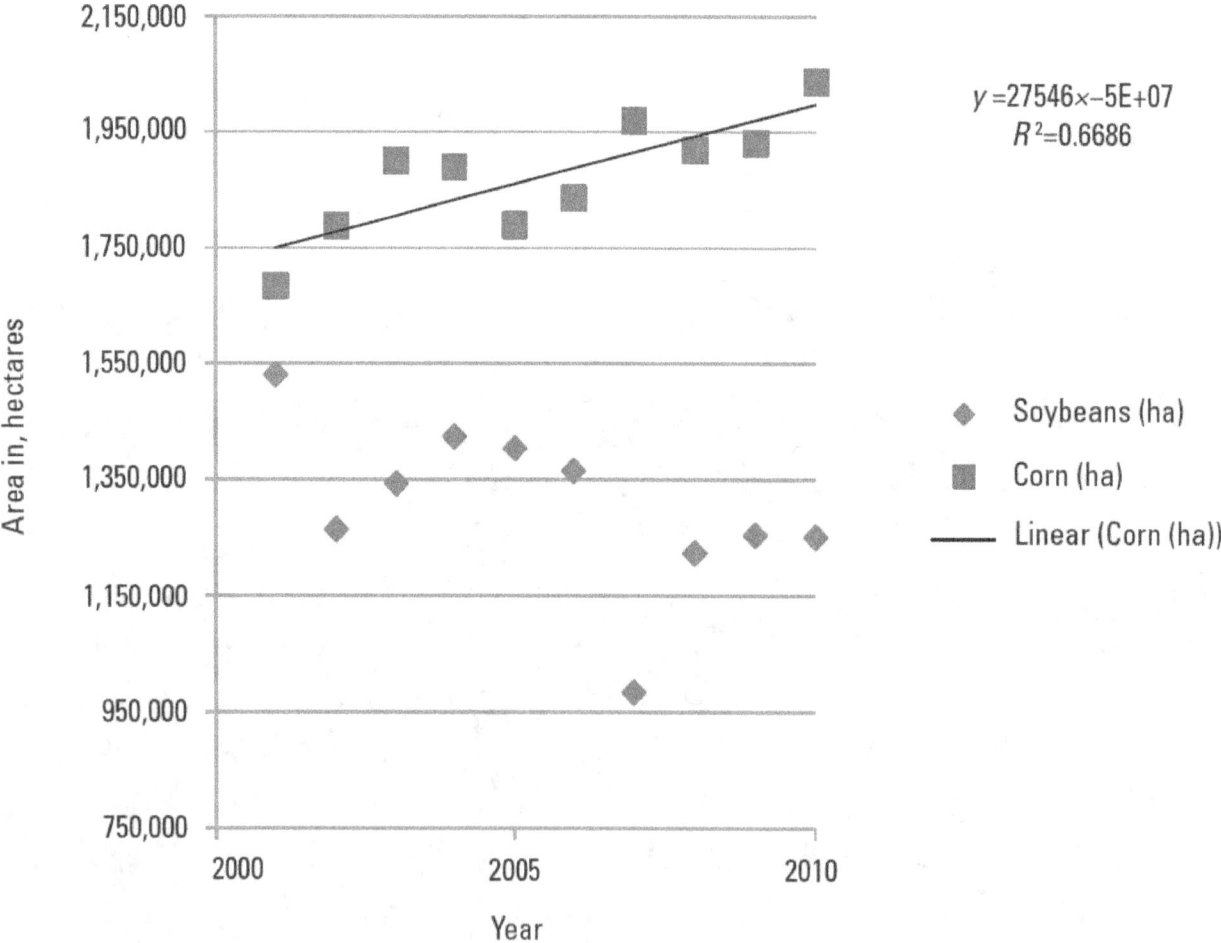

Figure 5. Graph showing trends in corn and soybeans in the 35-county northeastern Iowa study region, 2001–2010. Linear trend line of corn over time suggests an increase in area of production with more than 66 percent of the dependent variable's variation explained by the regression. Source data is from the National Agricultural Statistics Service's Cropland Data Layer.

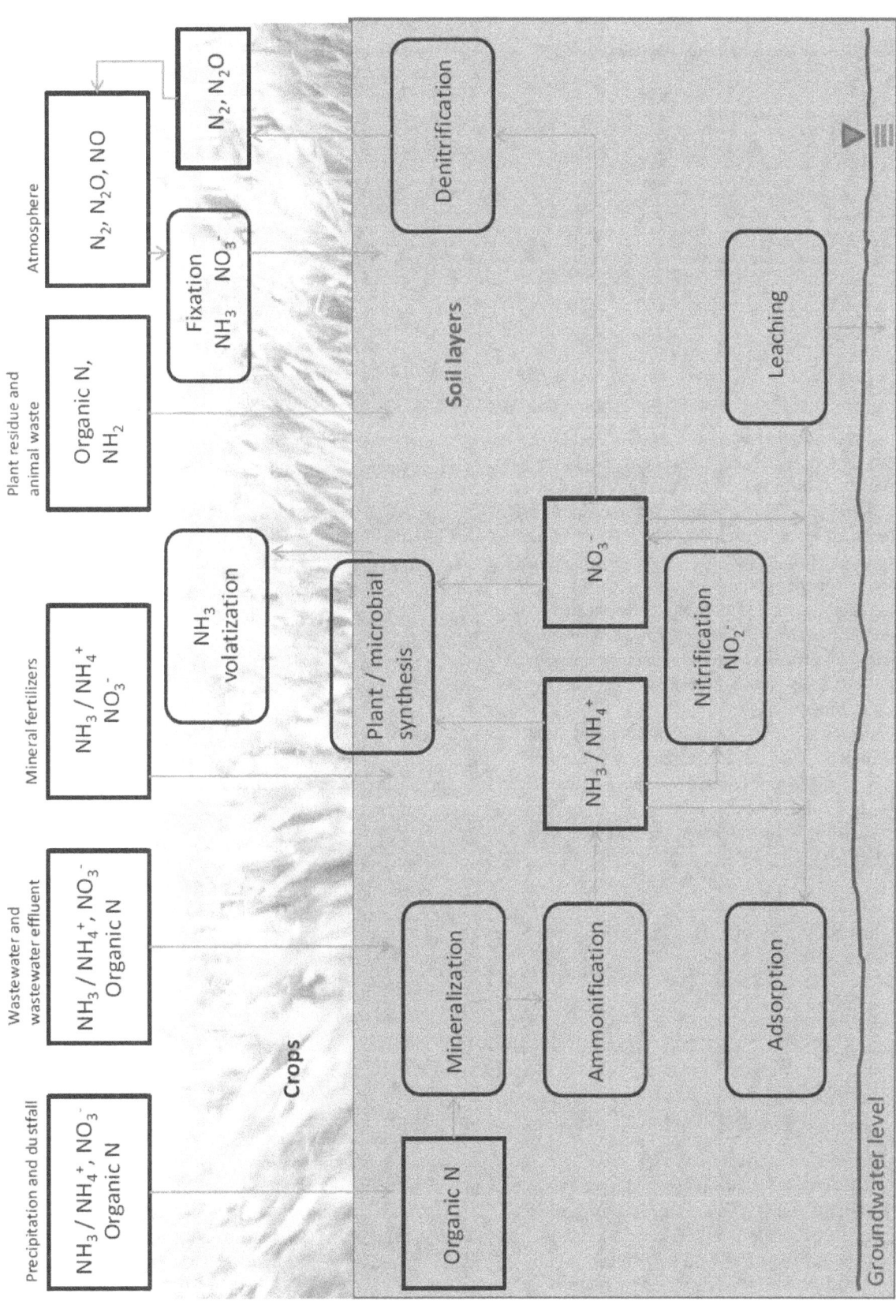

Figure 6. Diagram showing the nitrogen cycle. NH₃, ammonia; NH₄⁺, ammonium; NO₃⁻, nitrate; N, nitrogen; NH₂, ammonium; N₂, nitrogen gas; N₂O, nitrous oxide gas; NO, nitric oxide gas; NO₂⁻, nitrous dioxide. Modified from U.S. Environmental Protection Agency (1994), Canter (1997), and Brady and Weil (2002).

$$CNI_t = CNI_{t-1} + \sum_{i=1}^{T} (\Delta NO_3^-)_{t-i} \quad . \qquad (9)$$

The simplified equations for estimating concentration of nitrate in a well are:

$$CNI_t = \wp_0 + \wp_1 CNI_{t-1} + \sum_{i=1}^{T} \beta_i AC_{t-i} + \vartheta q_{th} + \varepsilon_t, \qquad (10)$$

$$CNI_t = \wp_0 + \wp_1 CNI_{t-1} + \sum_{i=1}^{T} \beta_i AC \times LF_{t-i} + \vartheta q_{th} + \varepsilon_t, \qquad (11)$$

$$CNI_t = \wp_0 + \wp_1 CNI_{t-1} + \sum_{i=1}^{T} \beta_i FAC_{t-i} + \vartheta q_{th} + \varepsilon_t, \qquad (12)$$

where $\wp$ is a regression coefficient, β is the estimate of the variables' coefficient, AC is the area under corn production in capture zones $t-i$ as discussed in the capture zone (CZ) delineation section, FAC is the fraction of corn production area out of total area in CZs $t-i$. AC and FAC were calculated using CDL for the years 2001 through 2010, LF is the leachate factor for the time period $t-i$ and is estimated using ArcSWAT as discussed in nitrogen leaching section, ϑq_{th} is the thickness of geologic Quaternary material, and ε is the regression residual. The simplified model accounts for time-variant variables, such as AC and FAC, and time-invariant variables, such as ϑq_{th}, across two spatial dimensions.

The CNI was initially estimated with the ordinary least squares (OLS) method. Using OLS to estimate CNI can lead to the possibility of having a problem with omitted variables. In this study, fixed effect models were used to account for omitted variables specific to wells. Therefore, the CNI equations were estimated as:

$$CNI_{j,t} = \wp_0 + \wp_1 CNI_{j,t-1} + \sum_{i=1}^{T} \beta_i AC_{i,t-i} LF_{i,t-i} + \qquad (13)$$
$$\vartheta q_{th} + \varepsilon_{j,t},$$

$$CNI_{j,t} = \wp_0 + \wp_1 CNI_{j,t-1} + \sum_{i=1}^{T} \beta_i FAC_{i,t-i} + \qquad (14)$$
$$\vartheta q_{th} + \varepsilon_{j,t}.$$

where j is a given well. Although a fixed effect model can correct the omitted variables problem, using a lagged variable as one of the regressors can cause an autocorrelation problem within the residuals. A standard approach in such a case is to estimate the regression equation with the Arrelano-Bond (1991) method, which assumes that residuals are not correlated across time. Arrelano and Bond proposed estimating

first-differences of both sides of the equations and use the lagged level as an instrument to obtain generalized method of moments (GMM) estimates. GMM is often robust in dealing with the violation of the assumptions of normality and homoskedasticity. The first-differences of equation 13 and 14 for the Arellano-Bond difference GMM estimation (one-step) method yields:

$$\Delta CNI_{j,t} = \wp_1 \Delta CNI_{j,t-1} + \sum_{i=1}^{T} \beta_i AC_{t-i} LF_{t-i} + \vartheta q_{th} + \varepsilon_{j,t}, \quad (15)$$

$$\Delta CNI_{j,t} = \wp_1 \Delta CNI_{j,t-1} + \sum_{i=1}^{T} \beta_i FAC_{t-i} + \vartheta q_{th} + \varepsilon_{j,t}. \quad (16)$$

The Arellano-Bond difference equation was also estimated using interaction term between AC and a Quaternary thickness categorical variable, where thickness categories were 0 to 15 meters (m), 15 to 30 m, 30 to 60 m, 60 to 92 m, and 92 m and greater.

Capture-Zone Delineation

In this study, we delineate individual CZs around specific wells that contribute to the fate and transport dynamics of nitrate observed in wells. Using the delineated CZs and the MRLI observations, the area under various land uses in the CZs of wells are estimated, which in turn is used to quantify nitrate contributed to groundwater pollution. Earlier research on groundwater pollution defined the CZ for water percolating from the land surface simply as a circular area around a well. For example Nolan and others (2002) used a circular area with diameter 500 m to model nitrate contamination in groundwater in given period, and Kolpin (1997) used diameters of 200, 500, 1,000, 1,500, and 2,000 m to assess the sensitivity of buffer size to land uses and groundwater contamination. The Iowa Department of Natural Resources (IDNR) made improvements on the circular-area delineation method for their wellhead protection program with the adoption of an ArcGIS version of an analytic elemental model (AEM) developed by the University of Buffalo (Silavisesrith and Matott, 2005). Given the difficulties of modeling flow paths in limestone and dolomite, both in karst and at depth, and in areas with inadequate data in nonkarst regions, the IDNR adopted conservative buffering rules of 1.60 kilometers (km) and 0.76 km in those cases. Otherwise, the IDNR used the AEM on a well-by-well basis, which included expert opinion on a case-by-case basis of flow directions, interactions among neighboring wells, and thickness of lithology (Chad Fields, IDNR, oral commun., 2011).

In this analysis, we specify the surface CZs for each time period t, using AEM (Strack and Haitjema, 1981) at a regional level. The AEM output assists with adequately characterizing the CZs in a given region, and constructs delineation areas essential for transferring this method to another geographic study region. The AEM software models regional groundwater flow and is used to delineate time-of-travel from annual CZs around individual wells (Rabideau and others, 2007). Also known as a particle tracking method, this simplified model attempts to account for complex hydrogeologic conditions (following Dupuit-Forchheimer approximation (Dupuit, 1863; Forchheimer, 1886)) to characterize three-dimensional (3D) groundwater flow in 2D models. CZs for wells in aquifers with negligible ambient flow are circular, whereas those for the wells with significant ambient-flow conditions can be comet or irregularly shaped as the horizontal influx of water through the hydrogeologic system creates the nonuniformity in geometric form of the CZ delineation. The radius of a circular capture zone for a well is calculated using a standard water balance equation (Haitjema, 2006):

$$r = \sqrt{\frac{QT}{3.14159(nb)}} \ , \qquad (17)$$

where r is the radius of capture zone, Q the pumping rate of well, T is the desired time of travel, n is the porosity in aquifer, and b is the thickness of aquifer. In the case of wells in an ambient-flow region, a dimensionless time parameter $\tilde{T}$ is calculated to distinguish whether the ambient flow is significant using the following equation (Ceric and Haitjema, 2005):

$$\tilde{T} = \frac{2(3.14159)Q_0^2 T}{nbQ} \ , \qquad (18)$$

where Q_0 is the uniform flow rate. If $\tilde{T} < 0.1$, ambient flow is considered negligible, and thus the capture zone is estimated as circular and stays as such up to $0.1 < \tilde{T} < 1$. If the ambient flow is large, in other words $\tilde{T} > 1$, the capture zone is irregularly shaped.

The annual CZs are delineated using the software, Split© (a software program using the analytic element to model single-layer groundwater flow in heterogeneous aquifers). The software was originally designed by Jankovic (2001) to delineate CZs for one time period for an individual well. Because of the regional focus of this work, the USGS automated Split to make an ArcGIS tool capable of efficiently delineating CZs for a number of wells (in other words, 300 wells were run in one batch) for a number of time periods across a large area (J. Jones and others, USGS, written commun., 2011). CZs were delineated using the USGS modification of the ArcAEM/Split model for the wells with known or derived hydrogeologic properties. Derivation was required because some of the hydrogeologic properties, such as thickness of aquifer and hydraulic conductivity, were not available for the wells. The thickness of two aquifers was calculated, and ordinary

and regression kriging was applied to interpolate a hydraulic conductivity surface (see appendix 3 for details).

Crop-Area Calculation Using MRLI

For the purpose of modeling the nitrate contribution to individual wells of particular fields across the 35-county region, a geospatial method was developed to calculate the corn/soy area in CZs over a 10-year period. The MRLI derived CDL from 2001 through 2010 was used to estimate the area of corn contributing nitrate to wells from their respective CZs. The CDLs for Iowa were clipped using GIS for the study region and were reclassified into four LULC categories—corn, soybean, other agricultural, and nonagricultural land use. The rasters were then converted into polygons. The annual CZs polygons for wells from the ArcAEM/Split model were then used to intersect the CDL polygons for each year to calculate the corn area in each CZ and marginal zones for each year. An example illustrating the area calculation is provided in figure 7 and area of corn for each CZ for a particular well (Jeanne Jones and others, USGS, written commun., 2011). Using the CDL data from 2001 through 2010, areas of specific land use—corn, soybean, other agricultural crops, and nonagriculture—were calculated for all the HRUs in the study region on an annual basis using ArcGIS 9.3 and ArcGIS 10 tools developed by the USGS Western Geographic Science Center (WGSC). This information was used to estimate dynamic nitrate pollution (or the *CNI*) to explain groundwater nitrate accumulation over time from changes in crop-rotation patterns.

Nitrogen-Leaching Estimation

Inorganic fertilizer and manure applied to agricultural croplands are known to be the most common sources of aboveground nitrogen loading to groundwater (Hallberg, 1989; Keeney, 1986). Studies of the amount contributed from different nitrogen sources vary widely (Ruddy, 2006; Libra and others, 2004). According to the county-level nutrient estimates by Ruddy (2006), farm fertilizer contributes 69 percent of the total nitrogen inputs to land as compared to 0.16 percent from confined livestock and 0.06 percent from atmospheric deposition. Another study by the Iowa Geologic Survey (Libra and others, 2004) of the State's nitrogen budget for 68 watersheds, which accounts for approximately 80 percent of the State, found that fertilizer accounted for 25 percent, manure accounted for 13 percent, atmospheric (wet and dry) deposition accounted for 16 percent, and disturbed (in other words, tilled or plowed) soils accounted for 26 percent. Although it represents a fraction of the nitrogen applied to a landscape, livestock wastes are used as nutrients applied to crops (Taraba and others, 1985). Because of the limitation of transportation costs, manure is often applied in the greatest rates in areas with high livestock densities (Greatz and Nair, 1995), which would include confined feed lots operations that help to concentrate manure and its collection. Hallberg (1989) states that the nitrate pollution associated with livestock feedlots is a localized problem. A study of nitrogen isotopes found that the primary sources of nitrate in sampled wells in Iowa were inorganic nitrogenous fertilizer (Schaap, 1999). Another study in Big Spring groundwater basin in Iowa shows a close correlation of increased nitrogenous fertilizer application in the region with the nitrate pollution in water (Libra and others, 1992). Therefore, we assume that the fertilizer-intensive agricultural sector is the primary driver of groundwater nitrate pollution in Iowa.

If a prior year's crop was corn and the current year's crop is corn, the recommended application rates for nitrogenous fertilizer before crop emergence is 170 to 225 kg/ha. If a prior year's crop was soybeans and the current year's crop is corn, the recommended application rate drops to 110 to 170 kg/ha (Iowa State University Extension, 1997). Over the period 2000 to 2010 in the Corn Belt, the Food and Agricultural Policy Research Institute (FAPRI) estimated an annual application rate of 163.1 kg/ha to corn production with a standard deviation of 6.0 kg/ha (Food and Agricultural Policy Research Institute, 2012). For soybeans, nitrogenous fertilizer is not required for growth because the plant is a nitrogen fixer; however, manure management plans have been shown to apply manure on soybean fields on the order of 100 to 200 kg/ha to facilitate volatilization and disposal of wastes (Jackson and others, 2000). Over the period 2000 to 2010 in the Corn Belt, FAPRI estimates an annual application rate of 23.3 kg/ha of manure to soybean fields with a standard deviation of 8.3 kg/ha.

After a crop has been fertilized and taken up essential nutrients for growth, an important consideration for this research is the amount of unused fertilizer that mobilizes as nitrate. As compared to the cation ammonium, which has a positive charge, the leaching of the anion nitrate out of the soil profile and into the subsurface hydrogeologic system is more likely to occur as nitrate ions are not adsorbed by the negatively charged colloids present in most soils (Brady and

Weil, 2002). However, in the lower soil horizons where pH is low, the anion exchange capacity is higher and can therefore adsorb nitrates. Given certain land-use types, management practices, soil characteristics, and geologic conditions (such as karst), the dominant factor determining the rate of leaching of nitrates from soils and into the subsurface is often the amount of water applied to the land surface—either as precipitation or irrigation—that infiltrates and percolates through the vadose zone (Canter, 1997). Another driving factor of leaching is the presence of minor topographic depressions under which leaching is more extensive (Fortin and others, 1991; Keller and others, 1988). Without accounting for tile drainage systems, in which a drainage network is installed under fields to dewater them for production purposes, this analysis is particularly focused on nitrate that migrates out of lower soil profiles and the bottom of the root zone as leachate.

To estimate leachate in this research, we employ ArcSWAT. It requires the inputs of topography, watersheds, and rivers (fig. 8), as well as soils (from the NRCS State Soil Geographic (STATSGO) database[9]) and LULC (from the CDL) to derive HRUs. ArcSWAT inputs climate (temperature and precipitation) from regional weather stations and, with crop rotation patterns and farm management practices such as fertilizer application established by the user, the model can run monthly to multiyear simulations to estimate leachate. From external sources of nitrogen and the remaining nitrogen not taken up by plants and crops, the estimated concentration of nitrate in solution is related to anion exclusion, soil porosity and water saturation, and the water balance among surface runoff, lateral flow, and (or) percolation. The amount of nitrate measured as nitrogen in percolation is estimated from the water volume and average concentration in the soil layer as:

---

[9]For more information on STATSGO see http://soils.usda.gov/survey/geography/ssurgo/description_statsgo2.html.

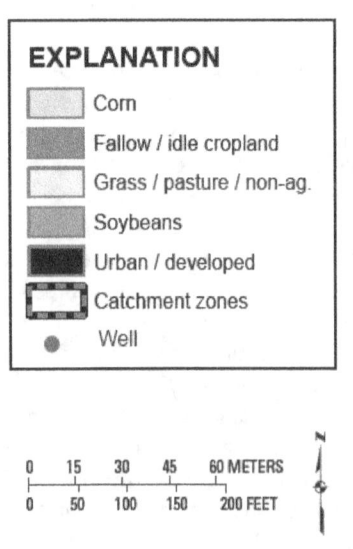

EXPLANATION

Corn

Fallow / idle cropland

Grass / pasture / non-ag.

Soybeans

Urban / developed

Catchment zones

• Well

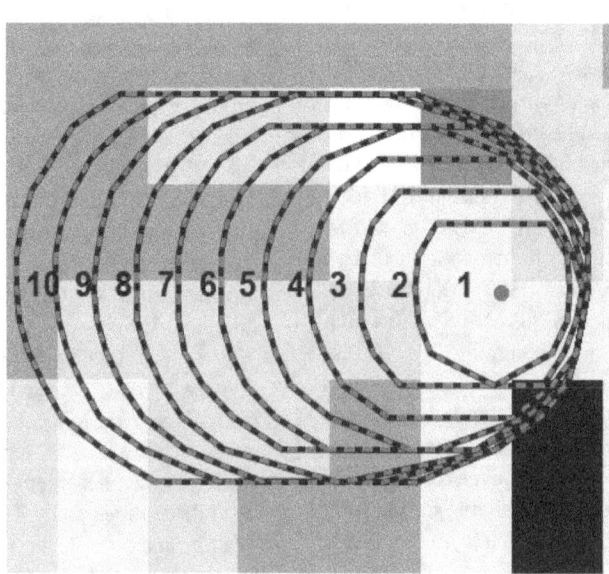

Figure 7. Map showing ArcAEM/Split model output and capture zone result on the National Agricultural Statistics Service's 2007 Cropland Data Layer (see http://datagateway.nrcs.usda.gov/). Non-ag., nonagricultural.

$$NO_{3p}^- = [NO_3^-] \times Q_p,$$ (19)

where NO_{3p}^- is the nitrate moved to the underlying soil layer by percolation in kilograms of nitrogen per hectare (kg N/ha) $\left[NO_3^- \right]$ is the concentration of nitrate in the mobile water that is moving through the soil layer in kilograms of nitrogen per millimeters of water (kg N/mm H$_2$O), and Q_p is the amount of water percolating to the underlying soil layers and aquifers in mm H$_2$O.

Leachate is estimated by ArcSWAT at the HRU level, of which there are a number for any given watershed or HUC. The user can define thresholds to define the number of HRUs within a HUC or watershed, which depends on the combination of LULC, soils, slopes, and the thresholds. In this work, the thresholds are set conservatively as 10-percent areal coverage for a given LULC (although all locations of corn and soybeans are included), 15-percent areal coverage for a given soil class, and 20-percent areal coverage for a given slope class.

Hazard Function and Groundwater Survival

Estimation of the benefits of MRLI involves estimating the cumulative groundwater nitrate pollution and fitting it into a groundwater survival model. For the purposes of this study, groundwater survival means that the groundwater remains potable with nitrate contamination below the MCL of 10 mg/L. The true state of contamination in space and time at the regional scale is unknown and can be only estimated with uncertainty. Thus, there is a need for a probabilistic model of groundwater vulnerability. Furthermore, modeling the survivability of an aquifer as perturbed by LULC changes provides an estimate of the vulnerability of particular land uses in specific regions.

Three major approaches to analyzing groundwater vulnerability exist—(1) overlaying of physical, mapped

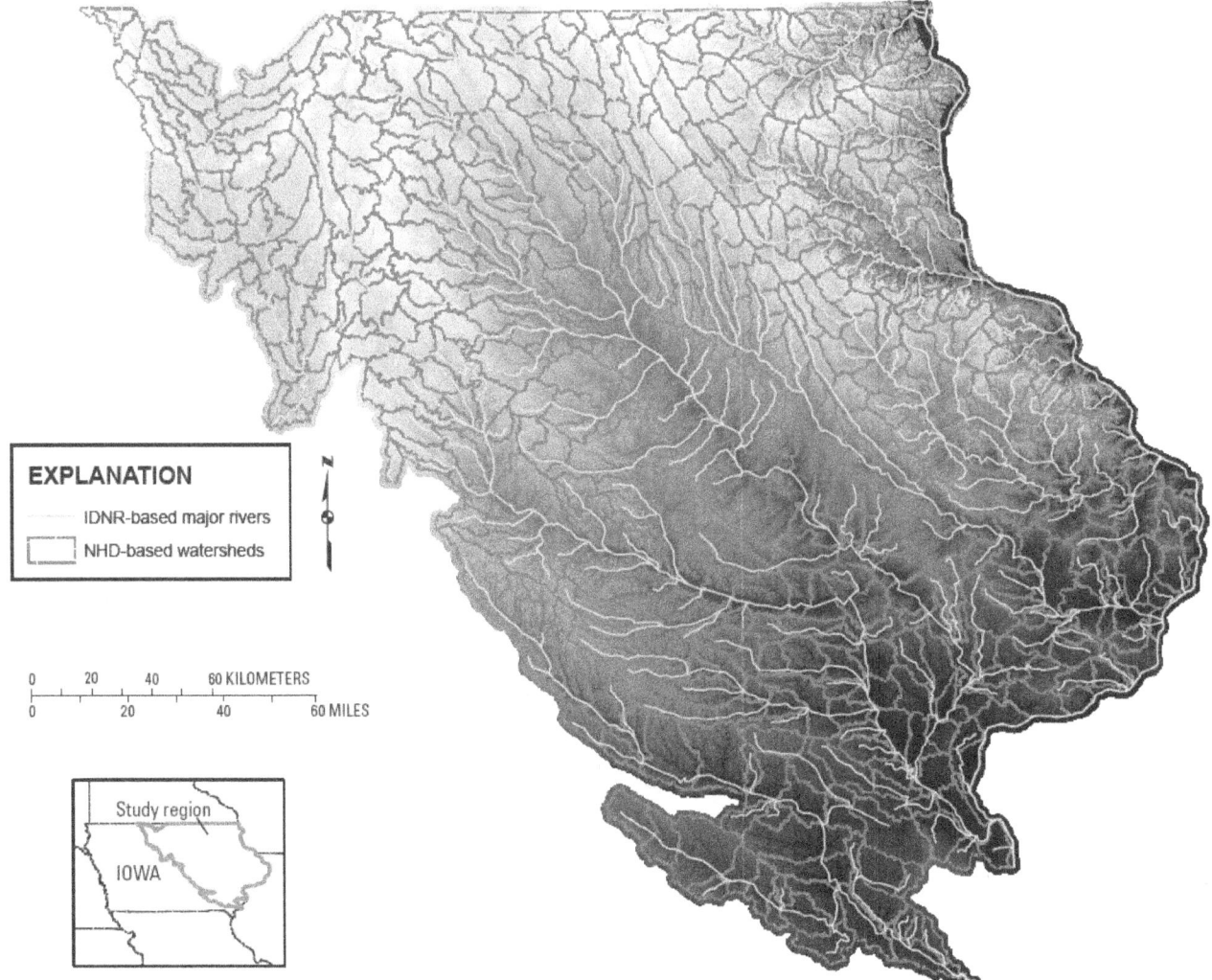

Figure 8. Map showing watersheds, rivers, and digital elevation model for the study region in northeastern Iowa. These geospatial datasets are also used as ArcSWAT inputs. IDNR, Iowa Department of Natural Resources; NHD, National Hydrography Dataset.

characteristics to create an index of vulnerability; (2) process-oriented methods using mathematical models to approximate subsurface flows, reactions, and dynamics; and (3) statistical methods where known levels of contamination are used to make inferences (Canter, 1997). In terms of the first approach, three problems are that the method (1) is not related to concentration, and thus the 10 MCL for nitrate; (2) does not account for significant heterogeneity in the subsurface environment, which would result in changing observed nitrate concentration levels at any given well; and (3) does not account for differential nitrogen loading at the land surface as a result of cropping patterns and management techniques (Canter, 1997). In the analysis we provide, the method relies on the second two approaches to create a series of models.

We apply a proportional hazards model to quantify the temporal risk of contaminating groundwater resources. The constraining risk we analyze is the risk of exceeding the MCL of 10 mg/L for nitrate contamination. The failure of a well is the event when the MCL is exceeded, and survival of a well is the condition where failure never occurs. In a proportional hazards model the probability of well survival, G (eq. 20), depends on the number of years, j, that elapse from any point in time a well is found to be in the surviving condition and the attributes of the well $\mathbf{x}_i$:

$$G(j|\mathbf{x}_i)=exp\left[-exp\left(\boldsymbol{\beta}\,\mathbf{x}_i+\gamma_j\right)\right], \qquad (20)$$

where $\boldsymbol{\beta}$ is the vector of parameters corresponding to the effect of well characteristics, $\mathbf{x}_i$, on survival and γ_j is the parameter quantifying the effect of elapsed time on survival.

We only observe the condition of a well, but the well data represent a sample of all of the aquifers analyzed, so this model can apply to any location in an aquifer. The attributes of the well include depth, CNI value, date, and location. The proportional hazards model provides a data field, which is applied in our study region to watersheds delineated at roughly the level of hydrologic unit code (HUC) 12 (table 1). HUCs are also termed watersheds and subbasins in this manuscript. Nitrate concentration is included among the well attributes through the CNI, so that crop types and plot characteristics are included as well. To assess the revealed social preference for groundwater risk that does not include explicit linkage to changing land uses and takes the current state of the landscape as a given, the nitrate concentration is part of that social preference choice described in equation 3 and therefore not included as an explanatory variable for survival.

We use all available nitrate groundwater concentration measurement data in the region that had the necessary attribution, of which we found almost 20,000 wells from the USGS

National Water-Quality Assessment Program (NAWQA)[10] and IDNR sources (table 1). This data in a well failure context is both right censored (failure occurred after a specific time but not how long after) and interval censored (failure occurred between two dates but not exactly which date in the interval), and because the data were not collected systematically for our purposes, the censor intervals are arbitrary (fig. 9). For example, a well i might be tested once and found in a surviving state and never tested again, so we conclude that it potentially fails in the future. Another well might be known to be in a failed state from every sample collected. Some wells are tested and found surviving and found in a failed state when next tested, so we know failure occurred between the time of these two tests. Some wells are found to survive multiple time periods before a test shows that it has failed, so we know both the surviving interval and the failure interval. Some wells are found to survive multiple times and never found failing, so we conclude that it might fail after the last test. Sometimes the failure is identified if it occurs in the subsequent time period when testing occurred in both time periods. The remainder of figure 9 illustrates variations of these categorical possibilities.

If we begin with a nitrate concentration measurement in a nonfailed well, we always have a lower bound on the failure time, so none of the data is left censored after eliminating failed wells. Some of the wells never fail, however, so if it is right censored we only know that the failure time is past the last well sample date. The wells that do fail constrain the failure time between the sample date when the nitrate concentration was first found to exceed the MCL and the prior sample date, so the data is interval censored. For some wells with high sampling rates, this interval consists of a single month, so we actually have an exact failure month, but for most wells, the interval consists of several possible failure months. The censoring occurs because of a nonsystematic sampling pattern, so it is classified as noninformative censoring. The proportional hazard estimation method described by Finkelstein (1986) applies to the type of data we have. The log likelihood function for this method is:

$$L=\sum_{i=1}^{N}log\sum_{j=1}^{m}\alpha_{ij}\,exp\left[exp(\boldsymbol{\beta}\,\mathbf{x}_i+\gamma_{j-1})\right] \\ -exp\left[-exp(\boldsymbol{\beta}\,\mathbf{x}_i+\gamma_j)\right], \qquad (21)$$

where $\alpha_{ij}=1$ if j is in the failure interval for well i and 0 otherwise for N wells that might fail within m years. We used the method of Broyden, Fletcher, Goldfarb and Shanno (BFGS)[11] to estimate values of γ_j and $\boldsymbol{\beta}$ that maximize L for the well data.

---

[10]For more information on NAWQA see http://water.usgs.gov/nawqa/.

[11]See, for example, page 24 of Nocedal and Wright (2006) for a description of this optimization algorithm, which is based on the independent work of the four eponymous mathematicians.

Table 1. Description of data used for estimation of economic value of remote-sensing information in the northeastern Iowa study region.

[USGS, U.S. Geological Survey; NRCS, Natural Resources Conservation Service; n.a , not applicable; m, meters; *CNI*, cumulative nitrate indicator, LULC. Land use/land cover]

Name	Source	Scale/accuracy	Purpose	Comments
Elevation at the base of the aquifer and elevation at the top of the aquifer	Iowa Department of Natural Resources	n.a.	To derive the thickness of the aquifer; use in capture zone delineation and CNI	n.a.
Source water assessment and protection wells	Iowa Department of Natural Resources	Horizontal varies from 35 to 1,135 m	Used in depth interpolation, CNI and groundwater survivability	n.a.
Private well tracking system wells	Iowa Department of Natural Resources	Horizontal = +/- 25 m	Used in CNI and groundwater survivability	Includes information on construction, lithology, pumping and capacity, and water quality
NAQWA monitoring wells	USGS National Water-Quality Assessment Program	n.a.	Used in CNI and groundwater survivability	Includes measurements of nitrate
Cropland Data Layer	National Agricultural Statistics Service	30- to 56-m pixels	LULC, agricultural production, CNI input, ArcSWAT input	n.a.
Digital elevation model (DEM)	USGS	10-m pixels	ArcSWAT input	n.a.
STATSGO soils	NRCS	1:250,000 scale, 250-m pixels	ArcSWAT input	n.a.
Watershed boundary dataset	National Hydrography Dataset , USGS	Hydrologic Unit Code 12, scale 1:24,000	ArcSWAT input, ground water survivability reporting unit	Required editing of linework due to State boundaries and ArcSWAT input requirements
Major river network	Iowa Department of Natural Resources	Positional accuracy ≈ 570 m	ArcSWAT input	Required editing of linework due to apparent errors and ArcSWAT input requirements
Aquifer properties (porosity, hydraulic conductivity, and others)	Iowa Department of Natural Resources	n.a.	Used in capture zone delineation	n.a.

Value of Information Estimation

Effective policy formation requires knowledge about the behavioral, production, and technological responses to alternative strategies (Bernardo and others, 1993a). A full policy analysis was beyond the scope of the analysis in this report, rather we develop tools to calculate the most value possible using the MRLI information. This includes an abstraction from precise policies that could be used to achieve that possible increase in value. With these tools, the value provided by MRLI can be estimated by the incremental benefit of increased revenue from land with the use of MRLI without further deteriorating groundwater quality. The VOI is estimated as (1) the economic benefit stream of a net increase in agricultural production across a region without sacrificing groundwater resources and (2) how agricultural production and its environmental impacts may change with or without the availability of MRLI. This includes focus on using improved information from new technology (in other words, MRLI obtained from satellites), which allows for estimating the joint production of agricultural goods and environmental impacts with and without the inclusion of MRLI, is discussed further below.

Without MRLI Case

This study is a retrospective analysis of the 2001 to 2010 time period, which relies on observed conditions for production of corn and soybeans and observed groundwater quality in the study region as the baseline alternative. Because this baseline alternative did not use MRLI in the IAA applied in this research, we label this alternative the "Without MRLI" case. Effectively conducted at a county scale from sampled data, the reported crop patterns are the consequence of the policies, $R^*(\omega(0),\alpha)$, prevailing during the study period as are the observed crop values, $PQ^*_{R(\omega(0),\alpha)}$. The VOI of the "without MRLI" case is compared to the VOI of the "with MRLI" case. The regulatory constraint, α, is the observed outcome for aquifers in the study region assessed using NAWQA and IDNR well sample data to estimate the proportional hazard model as a measure of the risk to groundwater resources.

With MRLI Case: Enhanced Landscape Configuration

The with MRLI case, which leverages a technological advance, informs what portions of the landscape could (or

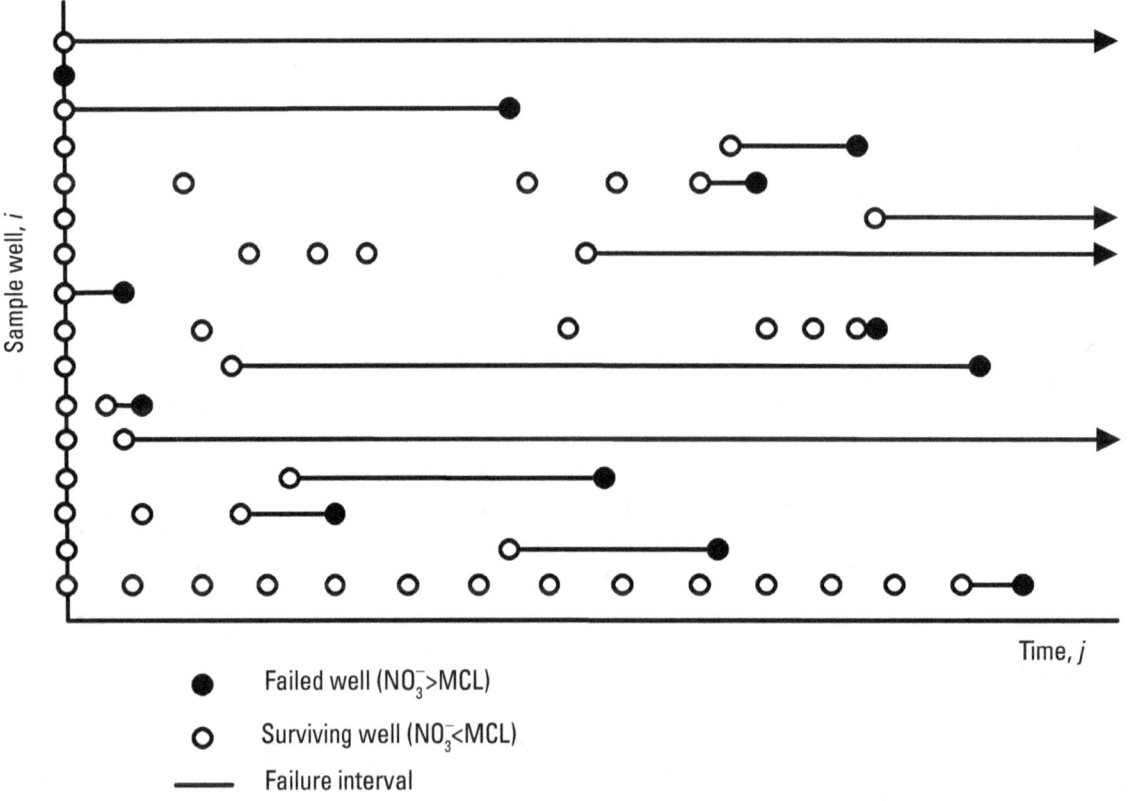

● Failed well ($NO_3^->MCL$)

○ Surviving well ($NO_3^-<MCL$)

—— Failure interval

Figure 9. Diagram illustrating arbitrarily interval-censored data used for the proportional hazards model. The proportional hazards model was used to quantify the groundwater failure process. Failure is defined as the groundwater nitrate concentration exceeding the Maximum Contamination Level ($NO_3^->MCL$) and survival is within the limit ($NO_3^-<MCL$). Groundwater samples were collected from wells in a pattern that was neither systematic nor randomized for the purposes of this analysis. Testing of the samples indicated either the well was a surviving well or a failed well, thus isolating time intervals in which the failure occurred as shown by the solid lines.

could not) support increased agricultural production, and leverages the improved information structure of MRLI. The social tolerance for risk levels can include scenarios of under- or over-regulation pertaining to groundwater contamination. This evaluation needs the spatiotemporal resolution of MRLI, and requires spatially explicit tradeoffs, optimization of land use, and (or) consideration of wall-to-wall regulatory restrictions.

In the empirical demonstration of the IAA, a useful exercise is estimating a nonpolicy specific solution to equation (1) or, alternatively, estimating a solution in which the policy instrument is the direct assignment of cropping patterns. This exercise is analogous to "central planner" analyses in economic growth theory[12]—the presumption is not that a central planner will actually make the choices but rather that we can establish a criterion to which we can compare the market based solution to solutions with alternative regulatory incentives and mechanisms. Thus, we are establishing a better possible outcome that we would seek to duplicate with a basket or collection of policies that decisionmakers could draft and (or) pass as legislation. Bernado and others (1993a) outlined various groundwater protection strategies available to policymakers, such as management-oriented, incentive-based, and regulatory alternatives. Regardless of the policy vehicle used to incentivize the particular changes in individual (microeconomic) and aggregate (macroeconomic) behavior, Benardo and others (1993b), took the approach of evaluating three activities—(1) the restriction of total farm nitrogen applications by one-third, (2) the restriction of unit-area nitrogen application by one-third, and (3) entirely eliminating the use of selected pesticides. Although the MRLI data were not used in the IAA to inform particular policies that would influence crop patterns, we outline how the method developed here can be used in considering economic incentive programs, policy rules, and location-specific changes in land management that could be brought to bear on developing a reasonable, enhanced configuration of the landscape. These methods can be used to additionally constrain the optimal allocation of land uses derived in the results of this paper to refine the current estimates of VOI, which would more comprehensively reflect the policymakers' decision space.

As an example of an IAA used as a DSS, Feng and Babock (2008) used an analytical framework that linked acreage allocation decisions with responses in total cropland area, which included adjustments in input usage, land-share allocations and total cropland area. Similar to the method used in our report, the authors also used characteristics of the land and its quality for production. They address the direct land-use changes that come from two sources—(1) cropland

put into corn production from another crop and (2) other lands taken from another use and put into crop production.

For our application, our enhanced landscape consists of identifying potential acreage changes to a baseline area of corn grown on each land type in each year of the analysis. From the enhanced landscape with MRLI data available, the case of the information structure not including MRLI data is subtracted (eq. 4). For the enhanced landscape configuration, the increase or decrease in corn area results in complementary increases or decreases in soybean area and implies changes towards an optimal pattern of LULC. The RATS (Regression Analysis of Time Series) linear programming algorithm (see below) was used to identify the optimal change in corn area for each subbasin land category. Practically, this direct assignment of crops in an HRU consists of choosing a corn/soybean cropland defined by satellite imagery and ArcSWAT and assigning an alternate crop choice. Given the history of crops for a watershed and other characteristics of the land in the HRU, such as soils and slope, both environmental risk and crop production are calculated. The solution is to assign HRUs within a given watershed with alternative crop choices each year until economic value is maximized subject to the environmental constraint. The HRUs are then aggregated within a given watershed. The binding environmental constraint is nitrate contamination of groundwater resources. We approximate the constraint by limiting the nitrate leaching to a level that does not worsen the risk that the groundwater resources will no longer be potable. Given what is known about locations sensitivity to nitrate leachate and groundwater pollution, the enhancement calculation is the choice of crop area assigned to corn or soybean for each land category in each HRU for each year of the analysis. The change in crop area combined with the estimated yield of that crop and its market price enables the calculation of crop value with and without MRLI that is used to calculate a VOI for each year of the study period (eq. 5). These yearly VOI values imply an EAI for the full study period and an NPV that would be possible if this same EAI is achieved in the indefinite future (eq. 6).

Materials and Data

In this section, we present details on the northeastern study region in Iowa, the MRLI-based, NASS-classified CDL, crop price data, well datasets, hydrogeologic characteristics, soil characteristics, slope and landscape topographic features, and rivers and watershed datasets. Groundwater vulnerability datasets were discussed previously. Data were collected (table 1), analyzed, modeled, and derived using various statistical and geospatial analyses tools in ArcGIS 9.3 and 10, Microsoft® Excel and Access, RATS (Regression Analysis of Time Series, version 7, ©2007 Estima, Inc., Evanston, Illinois) and STATA statistical software (release 11, ©2009 StataCorp LP, College Station, Texas).

---

[12]Using this technique Asada (2002), for example, analyzes the first best economic growth determined by a central planner and next finds a decentralized solution to compare real world mechanisms to the true optimum. Under free market conditions the solution is often shown to be equivalent to the central planner solution, but the central planner solution is more tractable.

EXPLANATION

Study region	Rye	Lentils	NLCD-open water
Corn	Oats	Peas	NLCD-developed/open space
Cotton	Millet	Clover/wildflowers	NLCD-developed/low intensity
Rice	Speltz	Fallow / idle Cropland	NLCD-developed/medium intensity
Sorghum	Canola	Grass / pasture / non-ag	NLCD-developed/high intesity
Soybeans	Flaxseed	Woodland	NLCD-barren
Sunflowers	Safflower	Peaches	NLCD-deciduous forest
Peanuts	Alfalfa	Apples	NLCD-evergreen forest
Tobacco	Other hays	Grapes	NLCD-mixed forest
Barley	Sugarbeats	Christmas trees	NLCD-shrubland
Drum wheat	Dry beans	Other tree nuts and fruit	NLCD-grassland / herbaceous
Spring wheat	Potatoes	Urban / developed	NLCD-pasture/hay
Winter wheat	Other crops	Water	NLCD-woody wetlands
Other small grains	Vegetables and fruits	Wetlands	NLCD-herbaceous wetlands
Winter wheat / soybeans	Watermelon	Aquaculture	

```
0    100   200 KILOMETERS
0    100        200 MILES
```

Figure 10. Map showing case study location in reference to the full extent of National Agricultural Statistics Service's 2007 Cropland Data Layer (see http://datagateway.nrcs.usda.gov/) for the Midwest. Red outline shows 35-county case study area in northeastern Iowa. NLCD, National Land Cover Dataset.

Northeastern Iowa Study Region

Shifting land-use patterns and vulnerable groundwater conditions in northeastern Iowa (fig. 10) makes this area an appropriate study site for the application of the IAA. The study region contains 5.4 million ha across 35 counties in northeastern Iowa overlain on aquifers of Silurian and Devonian age (fig. 11). The Silurian and Devonian aquifers are composed mainly of porous dolomite and limestone and shale, and are the most common aquifers in the study region. Typically in carbonate-rock dominated systems, porosity and permeability depend on fractures, bedding planes, and solution caverns, which can increase the relative rate of infiltration and percolation and the mobility contaminants. Such aquifers are often described as a single, large unit because the rocks making up individual units are similar in hydrogeologic properties and are hydraulically connected. Locally, shale and dolomites laden with clay act as aquicludes (Iowa Department of Natural Resources, 2003). The largest percentage of Iowa's farmland (76 percent) is devoted to croplands, with 92 percent of these croplands dedicated to growing corn and soybeans (Causarano and others, 2008). The State of Iowa produces 30 percent of the Nation's ethanol, and there are 42 ethanol plants in the State (Iowa Corn Growers Association, 2012). The CDL data for 2001 through 2010 shows a shifting land-use pattern from corn-soy crop rotation to corn monocropping in many parts of the State (fig. 12). In Iowa, 80 percent of drinking water is derived from groundwater, and the possibility of nitrate contamination in wells in the northeastern part of the State makes this area an even more compelling candidate for applying the methods of this report.

MRLI: Cropland Data Layer

For the 35-county study region, the CDL provided estimates of corn and soybean production from 2001 to 2010, which shows a general trend toward increasing corn production and decreasing soybean production (fig. 5). Because of the large ethanol production and typical crop-rotation patterns, the crops of interest are corn and soybeans. In the conceptual framework that was a precursor to this empirical application (Bernknopf and others, 2012), the authors characterized sensors (in particular Landsat, Advanced Wide Field Sensor (AWiFS), and MODIS) and proposed to compare the moderate-resolution land image (MRLI) information structure among them and traditional nonremote sensing techniques. If that approach were applied here, the length of record between Landsat (38 years) and AWiFS (5 years) and the distinctions between sensor characteristics would have been highlighted further. However, because of a number of reasons, the analysis undertaken in this study precluded the ability to classify raw imagery into a consistent, accurate LULC dataset. The most important reason was the lack of availability of historical ground-truth information. We approached the NASS about accessing the June Agricultural Survey (JAS) and the Common Land Unit (CLU), but the USDA agency does not preserve their historical records. Consequently, we chose the operational, standard data product of the highest known quality, length, and with the most relevant thematic LULC system, NASS's CDL. We also contracted with the University of Pennsylvania in an attempt to classify additional Landsat-based LULC products, the success of which is described below.

In Iowa, the NASS's CDL has been produced since 2000, yet the standardized nature of their product has fluctuated (fig. 12, table 2). From 2000 to 2005, the sole data source was Landsat. Because of the problems with the Scan Line Corrector of Landsat 7, NASS switched data sources to AWiFS and Moderate-resolution Imaging Spectroradiometer (MODIS) for the years 2006 to 2008. Johnson (2008) found that AWiFS was a valid alternative to Landsat-5 for agricultural regions with larger field sizes, and AWiFS offered the added benefits of larger swath widths and shorter revisit frequencies. For the 2009 and 2010 years, NASS switched again to include all three data sources (Landsat, AWiFS, and MODIS). Thus, there is no standardized product for analysis of the problem. Additional fluctuations include ground-truth data (JAS until 2006, then CLU to present), changing classification algorithms to derive the product (maximum classifier until 2006, then decision-tree classifier to present), software platforms (in-house NASS software techniques with Peditor until 2006 and then ERDAS, Inc., Imagine), annual error accuracies and metrics (table 2, for crops of interest), and output cell size (30 m until 2006, 56 m from 2006 to 2008, and then 30 m again in 2009 and 2010).

Depending on the year, the resolution or pixel size of the data is 30 or 56 m (Johnson and Mueller, 2010). The larger swath widths of AWiFS resulted in fewer scenes needing to be collected (State analysis districts in table 2). Table 2 characterizes the accuracies of the datasets for 2000 through 2010, which are important to keep in mind when they are used in further analysis. In comparing sensor characteristics and Landsat-based and AWiFS-based classification results, the change in pixel size has been shown to have the highest sensitivity to changes in accuracies (Johnson, 2008). In general, the accuracies from 2000 to 2006 for corn land-cover types were 87–97 percent and for soybeans were 86–98 percent. From 2007 to 2010, producer and user accuracies for corn land-cover types were 96–98 percent and 97–98 percent, respectively. During the same period, producer and user accuracies for soybean land-cover types were 95–97 percent and 95–98 percent, respectively. The errors include misclassification; for example, spot-checking certain pixels classified as corn within an urban setting with aerial photography suggested that the land cover was actually residential landscaping, and spot checking pixels classified as pasture showed that they were actually pavement.

As a result of the gap in Landsat imagery as source data for the CDL, we contracted the Wharton Geospatial Initiative

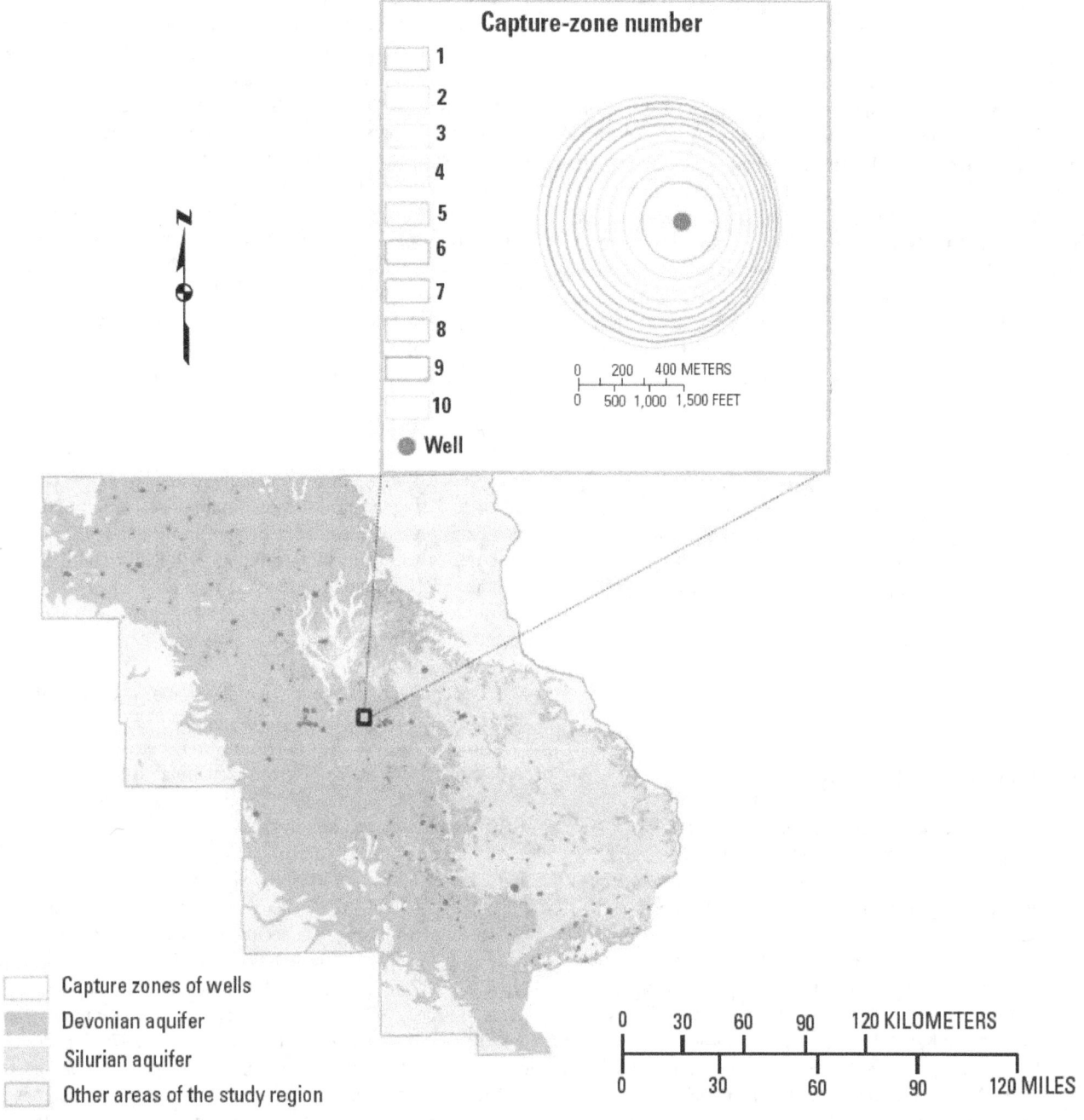

Figure 11.   Map showing the distribution of capture zones (CZs) delineated using ArcAEM/Split for the northeastern Iowa study region, which includes 35 counties. The CZs are used for calculating annual nitrogen loading in the cumulative nitrate indicator. The inset map shows the CZs for a particular well and their annual location during a 10-year period.

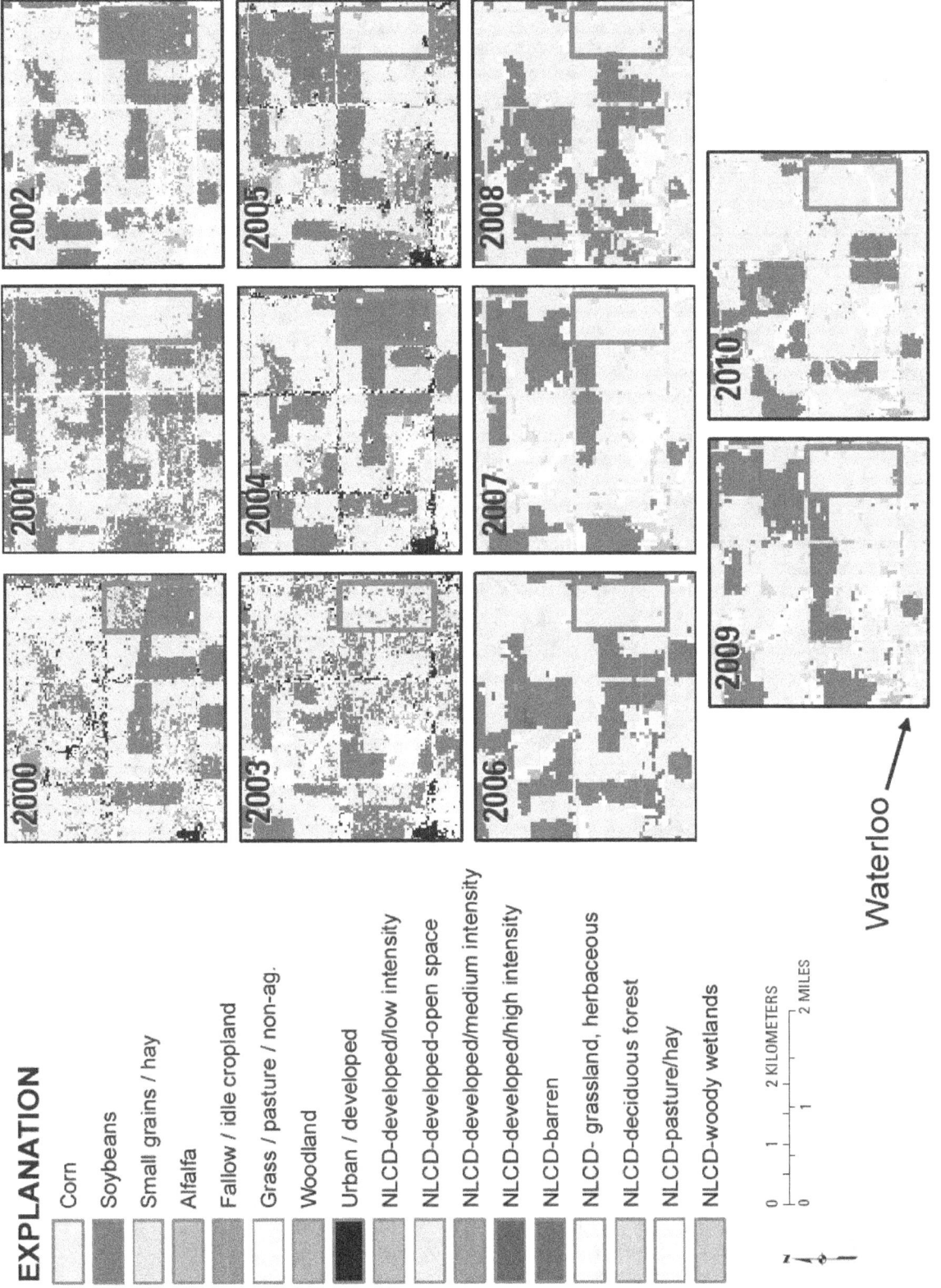

EXPLANATION

- Corn
- Soybeans
- Small grains / hay
- Alfalfa
- Fallow / idle cropland
- Grass / pasture / non-ag.
- Woodland
- Urban / developed
- NLCD-developed/low intensity
- NLCD-developed-open space
- NLCD-developed/medium intensity
- NLCD-developed/high intensity
- NLCD-barren
- NLCD- grassland, herbaceous
- NLCD-deciduous forest
- NLCD-pasture/hay
- NLCD-woody wetlands

Figure 12. Map showing crop rotation patterns with the National Agricultural Statistics Service's 2007 Cropland Data Layer (see http://datagateway.nrcs. usda.gov/) in a small part of the northeastern Iowa study region, which includes the City of Waterloo, 2000–2010. Note area highlighted in blue and the change in crop rotations after 2005. NLCD, National Land Cover Database. non-ag., nonagricultural.

Table 2. Shifting imaging sensors, accuracies, and metrics of the National Agricultural Statistics Service's Cropland Data Layer, 2000–2010.

[By convention, producer's accuracy and omission error always sum to 1.0, as do the User's Accuracy and Commission Error. Source: CDL metadata 2000 to 2010 (available at http://datagateway.nrcs.usda.gov). Imaging sensors—Landsat, Advanced Wide Field Sensor (AWiFS), Moderate-resolution Imaging Spectroradiometer (MODIS). avg., average; pct., percent; n.a., not applicable]

Accuracies and metrics	Landsat (2000–2005)						AWiFS/MODIS (2006–2008)			Landsat/AWiFS/ MODIS (2009–2010)	
Year	2000	2001	2002	2003	2004	2005	2006	2007	2008	2009	2010
State analysis districts	4	8	9	8	6	5	2	1	1	1	1
Corn											
Percent correct (avg.)	96.59	87.47	95.26	93.35	96.10	93.82	87.53	n.a.	n.a.	n.a.	n.a.
Commission error (pct. avg.)	6.90	9.38	5.74	4.64	1.58	3.27	7.19	n.a.	n.a.	n.a.	n.a.
Kappa coefficient (avg.)	94.16	80.61	92.55	88.43	93.03	88.59	77.53	n.a.	n.a.	n.a.	n.a.
Producer's accuracy (pct.)	n.a.	n.a.	n.a.	n.a.	n.a.	n.a.	n.a.	97.53	96.58	97.85	96.62
Omission error (pct.)	n.a.	n.a.	n.a.	n.a.	n.a.	n.a.	n.a.	2.47	3.42	2.15	3.38
Kappa coefficient	n.a.	n.a.	n.a.	n.a.	n.a.	n.a.	n.a.	0.95	0.92	0.95	0.93
User's accuracy (pct.)	n.a.	n.a.	n.a.	n.a.	n.a.	n.a.	n.a.	97.57	97.86	98.13	97.55
Commission error (pct.)	n.a.	n.a.	n.a.	n.a.	n.a.	n.a.	n.a.	2.43	2.14	1.87	2.45
Conditional kappa	n.a.	n.a.	n.a.	n.a.	n.a.	n.a.	n.a.	0.95	0.95	0.96	0.95
Soy											
Percent correct (avg.)	92.11	88.69	94.26	93.21	98.32	94.42	86.90	n.a.	n.a.	n.a.	n.a.
Commission error (pct. avg.)	5.69	9.60	3.76	7.03	3.84	6.34	10.61	n.a.	n.a.	n.a.	n.a.
Kappa coefficient (avg.)	89.73	84.57	88.52	89.11	96.69	93.60	79.61	n.a.	n.a.	n.a.	n.a.
Producer's accuracy (pct.)	n.a.	n.a.	n.a.	n.a.	n.a.	n.a.	n.a.	97.02	96.24	96.95	95.75
Omission error (pct.)	n.a.	n.a.	n.a.	n.a.	n.a.	n.a.	n.a.	2.98	3.76	3.05	4.25
Kappa coefficient	n.a.	n.a.	n.a.	n.a.	n.a.	n.a.	n.a.	0.96	0.94	0.95	0.93
User's accuracy (pct.)	n.a.	n.a.	n.a.	n.a.	n.a.	n.a.	n.a.	96.74	95.78	97.74	97.32
Commission error (pct.)	n.a.	n.a.	n.a.	n.a.	n.a.	n.a.	n.a.	3.26	4.22	2.26	2.68
Conditional kappa	n.a.	n.a.	n.a.	n.a.	n.a.	n.a.	n.a.	0.96	0.93	0.96	0.96

at the University of Pennsylvania in an attempt to classify the period of 2006 to 2008 with Landsat data. Given the lack of ground-truth data, the effort was marginally successful and had an error rate of about 15 to 22 percent (depending on the year) distinguishing between corn and soybeans (Amos and others, 2010). As a result—and in spite of data processing changes and accuracies that have been noted above—we decided to continue to use the CDL for the temporal and spatial characterization of LULC in the empirical application of the research project as it was the best available dataset. In working with the CDL, we also discovered that a part of Iowa within our study area in the 2000 CDL had not been classified, producing a data gap in our analysis that required our time series to begin in 2001. Most importantly, the CDL was able to provide LULC on an annual basis. For the purpose of our analysis and its focus on corn and soybeans, we simplified the extensive thematic CDL LULC classes into four classes—corn, soybeans, other agricultural, and nonagriculture. Although our models

and analyses use these mapped corn and soybean classification results in multiple ways, it should be noted that they are not absolute, deterministic cover types, and a level of uncertainty must be associated with them.

Crop Price Data

The analysis is restricted to marginal changes in production of two commodities; corn grain and soybeans. Thus, the price of these commodities during the period of analysis is crucial to the calculation of market values in this study. Data from the monthly Agricultural Prices reports (National Agricultural Statistics Service, 2012) are the basis for the commodity price data. Primary price survey data for these reports are collected each month as a randomized sampling of prices received by producers from virtually all mills and elevators that purchase corn grain and soybeans in the United States. Grain for seed is excluded from this data. The sales volumes are used to estimate a national average and a yearly average that correspond to the value of the cumulative crop. We used the annual average price received as the value of the commodities, which assumes (1) any modeled difference in sales of grain produced will be sold following the same pattern as the observed sales, (2) shifts in the market supply curve are small enough that we can ignore the change in equilibrium price, and (3) the difference between local and national prices are negligible. We deflated the prices to a real level (2010 prices) using the consumer price index for all urban consumers (CPI-U) U.S. city average of all items (Bureau of Labor Statistics, 2012). All values in this report are expressed in real terms at the 2010 price level. The real prices received for corn and soybeans (fig. 13) exhibit a declining trend until about the end of the past century and have continued to increase since then.

Wells

Data on physical properties and water quality of wells (table 1, fig. 14) in Silurian, Devonian, and Ordovician

aquifers in the study region were collected from IDNR and NAWQA. The observations from these wells are used in both the application of the *CNI*, as well as the aquifer vulnerability and time to failure models. Our comprehensive database of more than 35,000 wells integrates numerous disparate datasets and sources of wells and their characteristics. This included reprojecting geospatial datasets to consistent projection; mapping tabular data with latitude and longitude coordinates; calculating nearest neighbor distances as a spatial threshold for possible duplicate observations; joining (tabular and spatial), merging, and unioning multiple datasets in logical, sequential steps into a single geodatabase; clipping datasets to the 35-county study region; and deleting unnecessary fields and duplicate records.

The wells' depths range from just below the surface to 1,220 m, with an average depth of more than 50 m and a standard deviation of approximately 40 m (see Iowa Department of Natural Resources, table 1). This is in contrast to southern and western Iowa where approximately 52 percent of domestic wells are less than 15 m deep and are contained within sandy

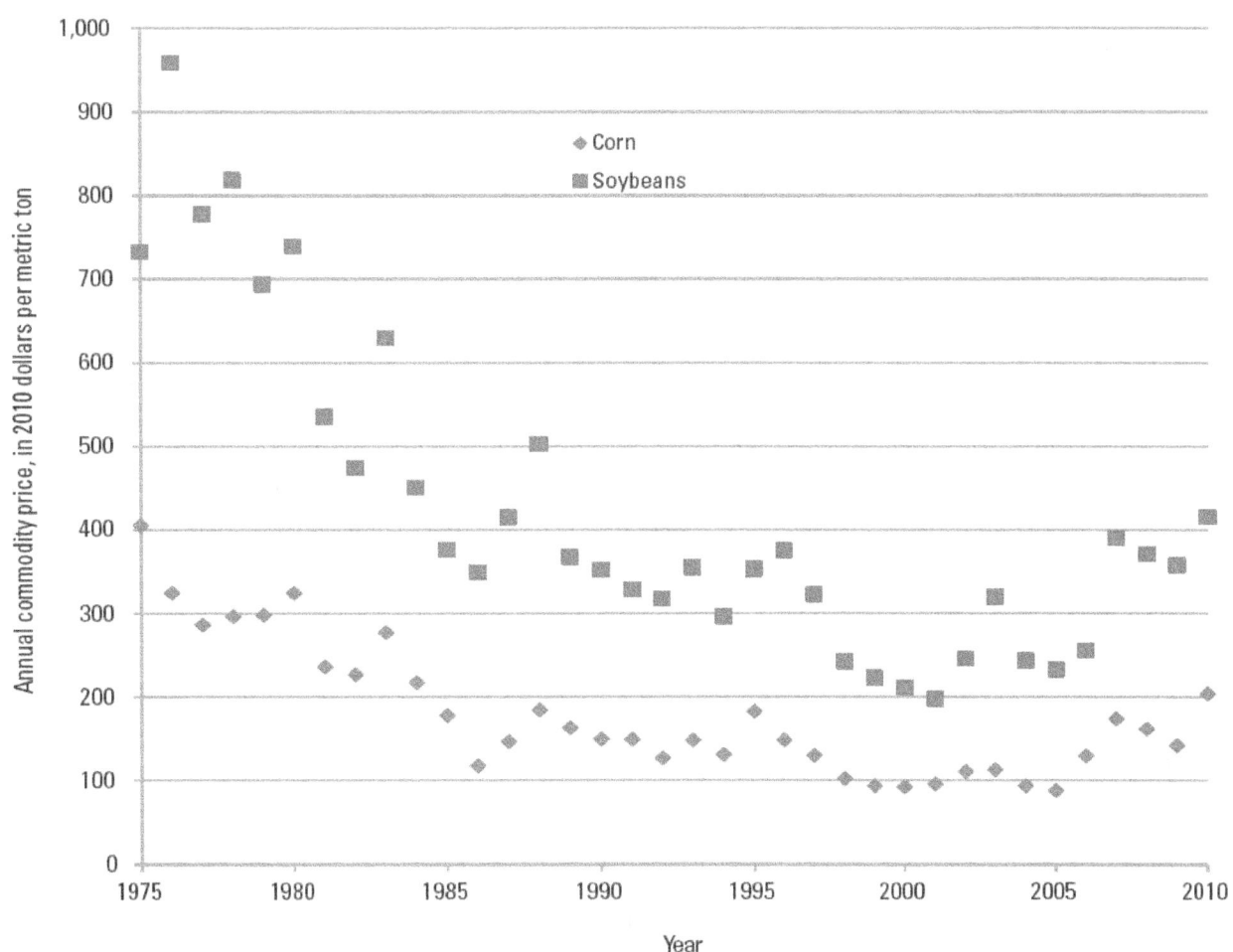

Figure 13. Graph showing average annual real prices received for corn grain and soybeans by U.S. producers. The data are derived from the monthly Agricultural Prices reports of the National Agricultural Statistics Service, Agricultural Statistics Board, U.S. Department of Agriculture. Prices deflated to the 2010 real level using the U.S. Department of Labor Bureau of Labor Statistics consumer price index for all urban consumers U.S. city average of all items.

drift zones of glacial-till deposits (Kross and others, 1990). An interpolated surface of more than 32,000 well depths shows a trend of (1) deeper wells in the northeast and (2) shallower wells in the north-south band in the middle of the study area (fig. 15). From more than 7,500 wells tested at various times, water yields average more than 139 liters per minute (L/min.) with a standard deviation of 359 L/min. (see Iowa Department of Natural Resources, table 1). For more than 2,900 wells, the measured values for hydraulic conductivity averaged 11.6 m per day (mpd) with a standard deviation of 52.5 mpd (see Iowa Department of Natural Resources, table 1).

Hydrogeologic Characteristics

Heterogeneity in the hydrogeologic properties of the northeastern Iowa study region that govern the nitrate dynamics in the aquifers include the thickness of the Quaternary

materials, aquifer characteristics, and well characteristics. The thicknesses of Quaternary materials range from 0 to 198 m in the study region (IDNR database). Aquifers in these Quaternary materials below 92 m are less likely to be impacted by leached nitrate (Robert Libra, IDNR, oral commun.). Therefore, a spatial-data layer for the thicknesses of Quaternary deposits in the study area was created for following thickness ranges: 0 to 15 m, 15 to 30 m, 30 to 60 m, 60 to 92 m, and 92 m and greater.

Data on aquifer characteristics such as type of aquifer, thickness of aquifer, flow direction, gradient, and hydraulic conductivity, as well as well characteristics such as well production and radius, were collected and derived from the IDNR database. For the wells without information on aquifer properties, values for specific properties were derived using data layers and ArcGIS software. For example, thickness and hydraulic conductivity layers were derived from available data from IDNR. Thickness of the aquifer (*Th*) was derived as:

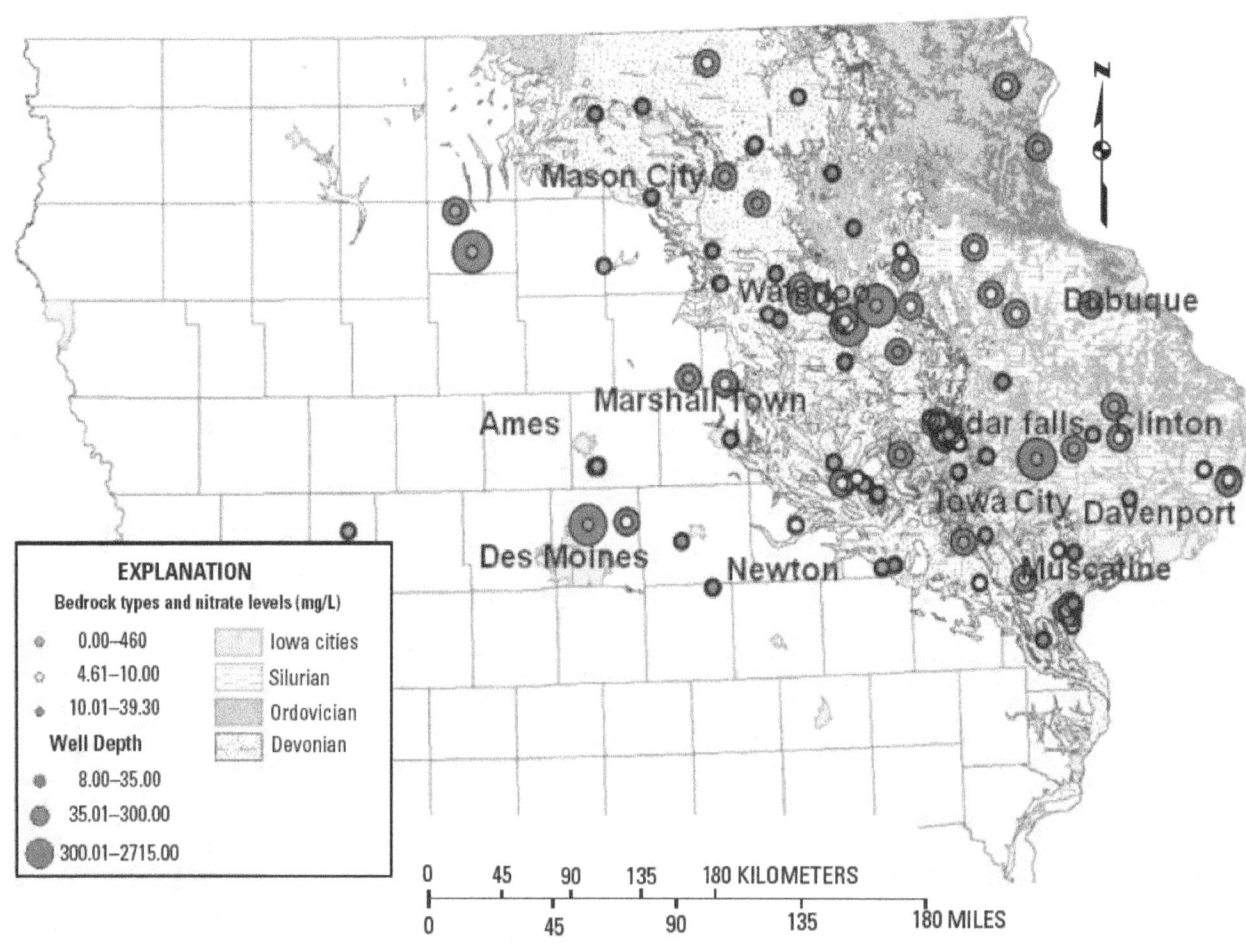

Figure 14. Map of Iowa showing a sample of National Water quality Assessment Program (NAWQA) wells in Silurian, Devonian, and Ordovician aquifers and cities in the northeastern Iowa study region. The sample includes nitrate levels found in the wells and their depths. mg/L, milligrams per liter.

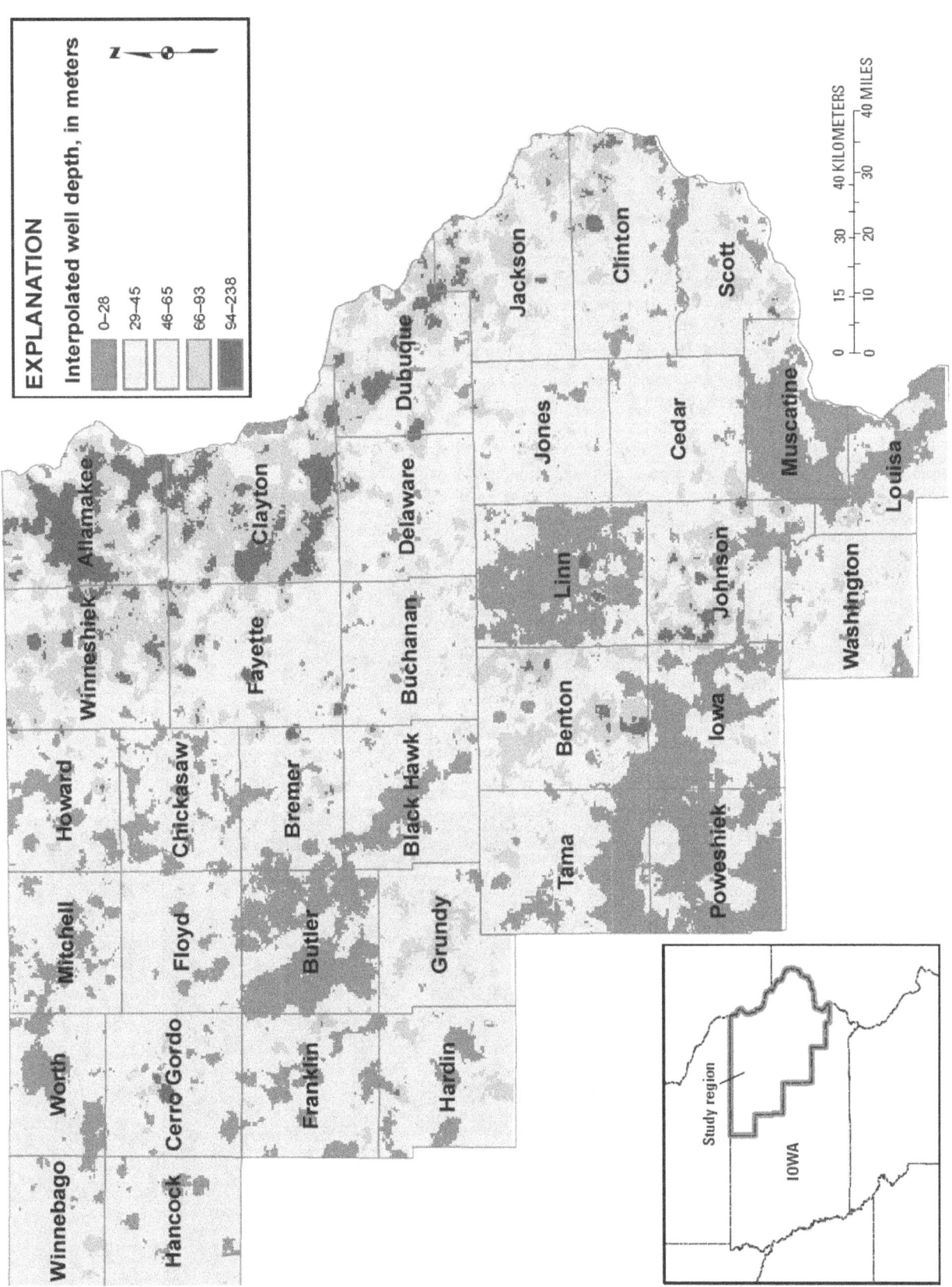

Figure 15. Map showing interpolated well depths for the 35-county northeastern Iowa study region.

$$Th = El_t - El_b, \qquad (22)$$

where El_t is the elevation at the top of the aquifer and El_b is the base elevation of the aquifer. The thickness layer was derived using GIS data and the technique of map algebra (ESRI, 2012) (fig. 16), and aquifer thickness for each well was calculated using spatial join in ArcGIS. A hydraulic-conductivity (HC) surface was created using the spatial interpolation method kriging (refer to appendix 3 for details).

Soil Characteristics

For the study area, the soils included in the analysis were related to natural boundaries, such as watersheds, rivers, and ridgelines. The NRCS STATSGO dataset was used (table 1). The soils database used in the analysis had a variety of important characteristics including hydrologic drainage group, texture, clay, silt, sand and rock content, number of layers in the soil, depth of specific soil layers, maximum rooting depth, moist bulk density, available water capacity, organic carbon content, saturated HC, and electrical conductivity.

Slope, Depressions, and Topographic Position

The USGS digital elevation model (DEM) of northeastern Iowa (table 1) and its shaded relief provides an insight to the topography and relief of the study region. We used the USGS 10-m DEM (table 1), and the 35 case-study counties had elevations that varied from 138.9 to 443.2 m above sea level (fig. 17). As mentioned previously, topographic characteristics play an important role in the fate and transport of nitrogen. For example, high slopes tend to have more overland runoff and lateral movement of nitrogen, depressions and topographic convergences tend to have higher levels of percolation and infiltration, topographic position along a hillslope and across a landscape can be related to water table depths, baseflow provided to rivers, and nutrient uptake dynamics along the flowpath to a river, canal, drainage ditch, or waterway. The ArcGIS version of ArcSWAT requires DEM inputs to calculate such watershed and subbasin characteristics. For the analysis, slopes were classified into 5 ranges—0–2 percent, 2–5 percent, 5–8 percent, 8–12 percent, and greater than 12 percent.

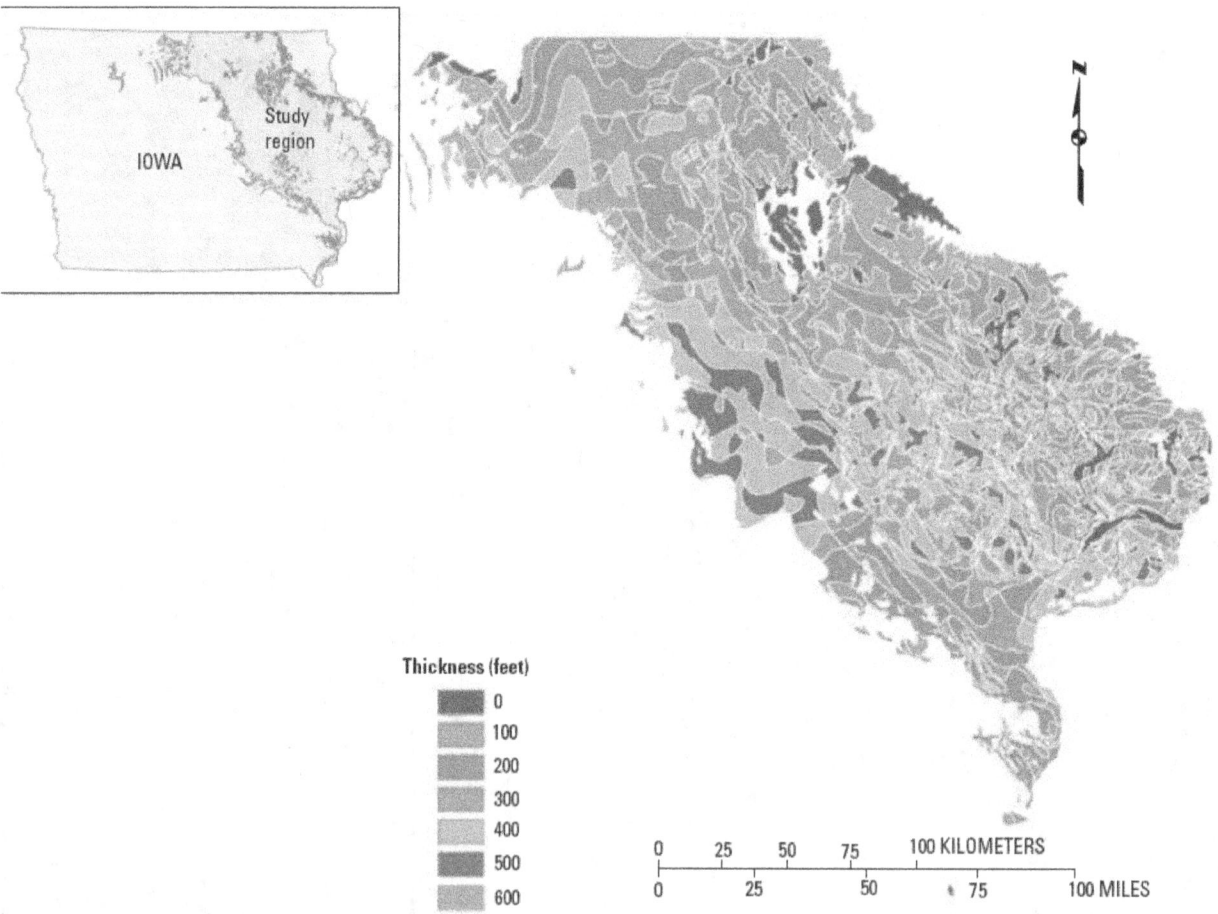

Figure 16. Map showing derived Silurian and Devonian aquifer thicknesses in the northeastern Iowa study region. Source is Iowa Department of Natural Resources.

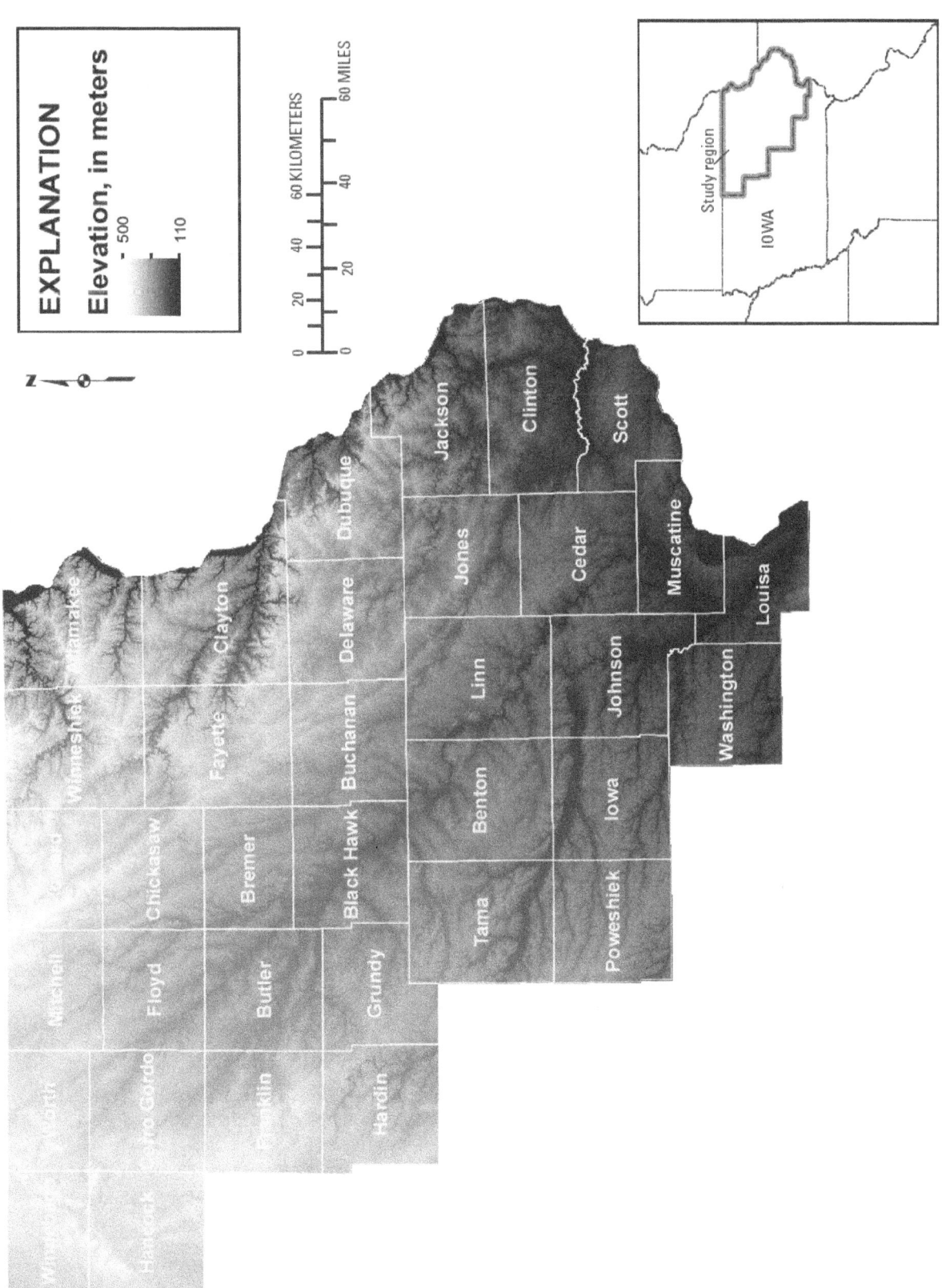

Figure 17. Map showing shaded relief of topography for the 35-county northeastern Iowa study region. Source is U.S. Geological Survey National Elevation Dataset.

Rivers, Watersheds, and Hydrologic Response Units

Although datasets are available and analyses are conducted at coarser and finer scales, this research is mostly organized into the spatial units of watersheds for reporting. The National Hydrography Dataset (NHD) Watershed Boundary Dataset HUC level 12 (table 1) is used as the starting point for delineating watersheds. Alterations to the watershed boundaries were made for the sake of conforming to the State of Iowa's boundaries, as well as for merging of HUCs that were not intersected by the river network. The case study has 603 watersheds and went beyond the extent of the anthropogenic-boundaries of the 35 counties so as to reflect more of the natural ecosystem processes. The river network was provided by IDNR and required routing and delineation improvements on the basis of the DEM. Also, because of the requirements of ArcSWAT, any given HUC could only have one river segment contained within it. For example, a watershed that had both a headwater stream originating in it as well as a higher-order stream flowing through it was simplified to preserve the inter-watershed connectivity of the higher-order stream network (fig. 8).

Results and Discussion

This section presents the results for the research on agricultural production, aquifer contamination, and VOI estimates. An overall discussion follows at the end of the section, which also considers avenues for future work and research efforts.

Agricultural Production

Annual simulations were run to estimate yield and area of corn and soybeans from 2001 to 2010. Results are reported at the subbasin level even though multiple HRUs were analyzed within a given subbasin. For the 603 subbasins, there was a median of 7,910 HRUs over the 10 years, with a standard deviation of 316. The total number of HRUs for all HUCs in the study region varies by year, with a range in HRUs per year of 7,758 to 8,813. The number of HRUs per HUC per year is in the range of 2 to 27. Yield estimates and area results are summarized by LULC and year (table 3). The area-weighted average of each subbasin's aggregated yield (corn, soybeans) from 2001 to 2010 is provided as well (fig. 18). The values are classified with the Jenks natural breaks classification method (in other words, reducing the variance within classes, while maximizing the variance between classes) and provide an indication of the overall agricultural productivity of certain subbasins over time.

Nitrate Contamination of Aquifers

In this subsection, we discuss the results of the dynamic nitrate-pollution models and analysis, the estimation of leachate, and groundwater vulnerability.

Dynamic Nitrate Pollution

Given certain hydrogeologic and well conditions, two shapes for annual CZs are expected to occur in the study region—(1) no subsurface flow will create concentric circles, and (2) the presence of subsurface flow will create irregular shapes (figs. 7 and 11). The *CNI* equations were estimated using nitrate levels (mg/L) observed in the wells over the period 2001 through 2010 and regressed on the previous year's nitrate levels (mg/L) by year leached quantity of nitrate (kg/ha) from each CZ and thickness of Quaternary material (m). The leached quantity of nitrate in each CZ was estimated as the product of area under crop (corn), and the nitrate leach factor (kg /ha) was obtained from ArcSWAT results for the well location. Area under corn in the CZ and the marginal zones[13] of respective wells were calculated for each well using MRLI as discussed earlier. The *CNI* equations were also estimated by substituting leached quantity by (1) the leached fraction, (2) area of corn in each CZs (ha), (3) interaction of corn acres in CZs, and (4) Quaternary deposit thickness (m) in the well location (table 4). The leached fraction is the quantity leached from the area that produced corn in the CZ divided by the total area in the CZ. Fraction of corn was estimated by dividing the area under corn by total area in the CZ. All of these area calculations depended on the MRLI-derived CDL.

Wells with two or more nitrate observations over the period of 2000 through 2010 were used in the *CNI* analysis, and 80 out of 350 observations showed decrease in nitrate level. The ordinary least square (OLS) estimation of *CNI* equations 10 and 11 are shown in table 5. The lags (previous year's nitrate measurement) for area and leached quantity have positive signs and are significantly different from zero suggesting that the *CNI* levels in wells are significantly affected by the input factors specified in the independent variables. The area under corn and nitrate leached from capture zones (1, 2, 3, and 4–10) have expected signs, however, they are not significant. Theoretically, the greater the thickness of the Quaternary materials, the lower the values of *CNI* in wells should be; however, the OLS results do not conform to it. The *CNI* equations specified with the OLS regression equation were estimated using the fraction of corn area in CZs and fraction of leachate in CZs. Most of the independent variables were statically insignificant, except for certain CZs (2 and 4–10) that in the fraction of leachate equation were significant at the 10 percent level, which may not have sufficient explanatory power as variables may have been omitted.

The Arellano-Bond estimation results shown in table 6 suggest that the annual change in nitrate level in wells is not significantly affected by change in nitrate level in the previous year for *CNI* equations 15 and 16. The positive signs and

---

[13]Marginal zones refer to the area in CZ of a well, from which left over pollutants from year $t-1$ are added to the well in year t.

Table 3. Crop yield estimates and area calculations for four land-use/land-cover (LULC) types of the northeastern
Iowa study region, 2001–2010.

[ag.,agricultural; non-ag., nonagricultural;HRU, hydrologic response unit; --, no data; t, metric tons; ha, hectares; km^2, kilometers]

Year	LULC type	Mean yield (t/ha)	Total yield for study region (t)	Mean total yield per HRU (t)	Mean area of HRU (km^2)
2001	Other Ag.	5.91	14,195,362.5	5,639.8	9.4
	Corn	7.46	11,067,551.9	6,369.5	8.5
	Non Ag.	--	--	--	8.8
	Soybeans	3.32	4,319,402.9	2,372.3	7.4
Total			29,582,317.3		
2002	Other Ag.	5.92	15,104,376.3	5,914.0	10.0
	Corn	9.75	14,302,940.1	8,059.1	8.6
	Non Ag.	--	--	--	4.9
	Soybeans	2.27	2,527,774.5	1,421.7	6.6
Total			31,935,090.9		
2003	Other Ag.	5.91	13,025,402.5	5,864.7	9.6
	Corn	9.74	16,255,344.1	8,461.4	9.3
	Non Ag.	--	--	--	4.9
	Soybeans	2.26	2,779,423.8	1,503.3	7.0
Total			32,060,170.4		
2004	Other Ag.	5.94	12,014,125.7	5,387.5	8.8
	Corn	9.73	16,387,295.2	8,649.5	9.4
	Non Ag.	--	--	--	4.2
	Soybeans	2.27	2,921,613.2	1,580.3	7.4
Total			31,323,034.2		
2005	Other Ag.	5.91	13,249,121.5	5,441.1	9.1
	Corn	9.75	14,983,288.1	7,974.7	8.6
	Non Ag.	--	--	--	4.7
	Soybeans	2.27	2,728,292.2	1,499.3	6.8
Total			30,960,701.8		
2006	Other Ag.	5.88	5,637,308.6	3,316.1	4.9
	Corn	9.75	16,370,874.0	8,519.7	9.4
	Non Ag.	--	--	--	7.0
	Soybeans	2.27	2,790,736.7	1,569.0	7.3
Total			24,798,919.3		
2007	Corn	9.74	16,540,934.1	8,817.3	9.7
	Non Ag.	--	--	--	10.8
	Soybeans	2.28	1,923,920.9	1,127.7	5.2
Total			18,464,854.9		

Table 3. Crop yield estimates and area calculations for four land-use/land-cover (LULC) types of the northeastern Iowa study region, 2001–2010.—Continued

[ag.,agricultural; non-ag., nonagricultural;HRU, hydrologic response unit; --, no data; t, metric tons; ha, hectares; km², kilometers]

Year	LULC type	Mean yield (t/ha)	Total yield for study region (t)	Mean total yield per HRU (t)	Mean area of HRU (km²)
2008	Other Ag.	5.96	81,694.2	1,633.9	2.9
	Corn	9.75	16,040,976.8	8,439.2	9.7
	Non Ag.	--	--	--	10.1
	Soybeans	2.28	2,363,372.7	1,330.2	6.1
Total			18,486,043.8		
2009	Other Ag.	6.06	89,295.4	1,594.6	2.4
	Corn	9.74	16,076,559.9	8,502.1	9.3
	Non Ag.	--	--	--	9.9
	Soybeans	2.27	2,448,455.4	1,404.9	6.5
Total			18,614,310.7		
2010	Other Ag.	6.00	537,593.7	1,576.5	2.4
	Corn	9.75	16,595,206.6	8,973.0	7.3
	Non Ag.	--	--	--	9.3
	Soybeans	2.26	2,409,897.8	1,368.7	6.3
Total			19,542,698.1		
Grand total			255,768,141.5		

significance level of the coefficients on quantity of nitrate leached from CZs 2, 3, and 4–10 suggest that an increase in corn area or the amount of nitrate leached increases the nitrate added to wells each year. The insignificance of nitrate leached from the first year CZ may be due to less or no corn produced in the area nearby wells, or it may be due to the lack of greater than 1-year-old water in the pumped well. The nitrate leached in 2nd-year CZ infiltrated water increases nitrate in wells more than by the nitrate leached in 3rd-year CZ infiltrated water. Results suggest that the *CNI* equation including the independent variable of leached quantity (eq. 15) performed better than the one using only corn area (eq. 16). The results show that the thicker the Quaternary material, the lower the increase in the nitrate level, as expected.

The results of the Arellano-Bond estimation of the *CNI* include using corn area and Quaternar thickness interaction terms (table 7). The estimations show that corn area overlain on as much as 15 m of Quaternary materials positively and significantly increases the nitrate levels in the wells, whereas corn area overlain on more than 15 m of Quaternary materials are not significant. Given this result of groundwater survivability improving in areas with thicker Quaternary materials, the allocation of agricultural production was better optimized to derived an estimate of VOI.

Leachate Estimation

Turning to the other product of the IAA's joint output, namely leachate, it was estimated using ArcSWAT. Similar to the yield estimates, multiple HRUs were derived for the estimates of leachate rate. Given that HRUs are not explicitly mapped, leachate estimates are reported at the subbasin or watershed level. Total leachate and average (mean) leachate rate are presented by year for corn and soybeans (table 8). The location and values of nitrate leaching rates are area-weight averaged to the subbasin level for the corn and soybean LULC classes (fig. 19). The values are classified with the natural Jenks method.

The agricultural production of corn and soybeans can have the ancillary impact of increased nitrogen loading, leaching, and percolation. Some studies have addressed leaching and percolation rates that can be directly compared to our results. Using four irrigation levels and three nitrogen application levels for maize crops, Gheysari and others (2009) observed at a 2-m scale nitrogen leaching rates of 0.0 to 8.4 kg/ha, with higher values related to land-use treatments of high fertilization and over irrigation. Using 2.4-m deep lysimeters, Owens and others (1994) measured mean annual nitrogen leaching rates of 31.6 to 47.1 kg/ha during a 6-year study in eastern Iowa of corn and soybean rotation.

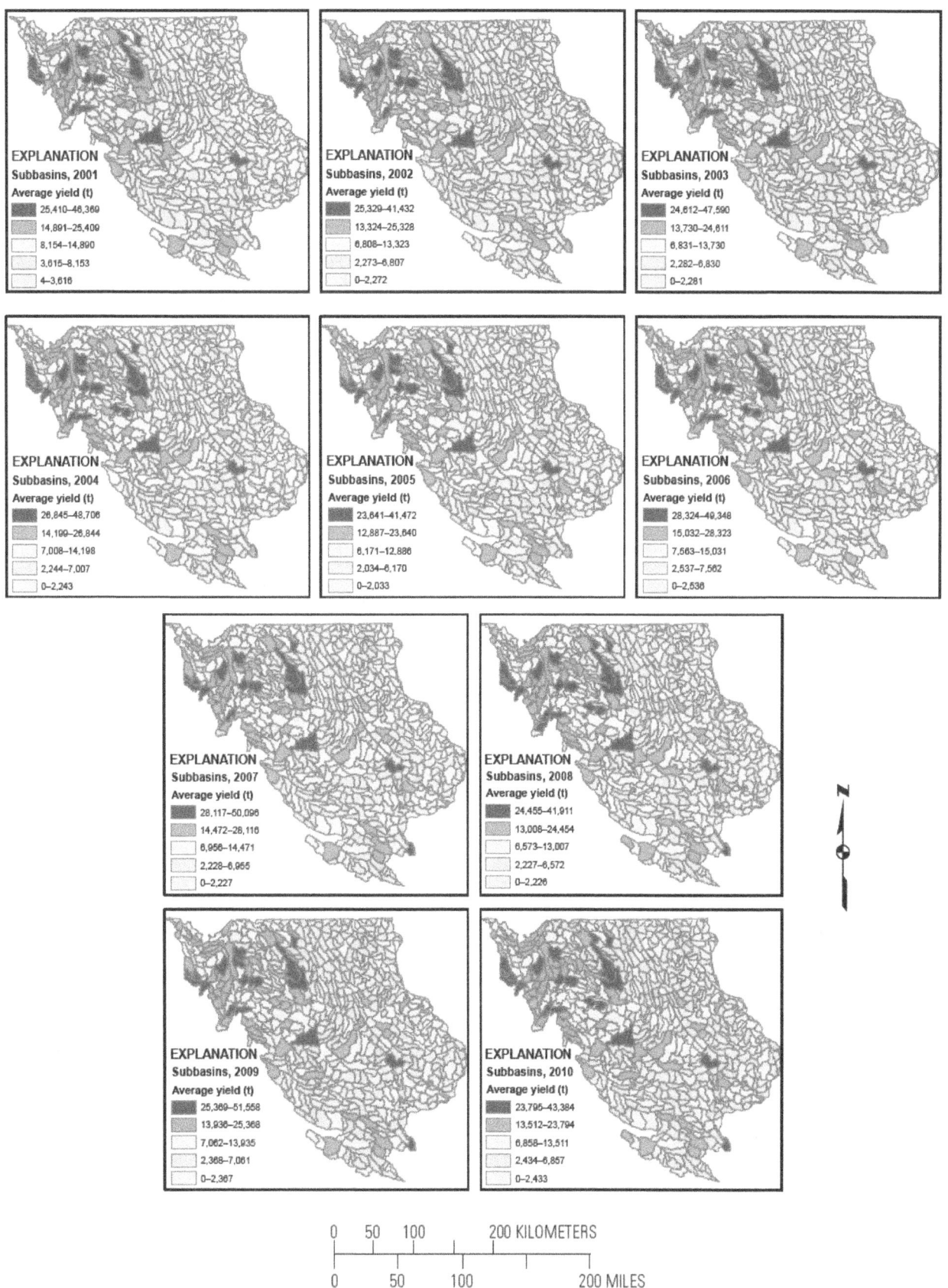

Figure 18. Subbasin-level yield maps for combined corn and soybean production estimated from ArcSWAT for the northeastern Iowa study region, 2001 to 2010. t, metric ton.

Table 4. Summary statistics for cumulative nitrate indicator (*CNI*) data.

[Std. dev., standard deviation; Min, minimum; Max, maximum; CZ, capture zone; mg/L, milligrams per liter; ha, hectares; kg/ha, kilograms per hectare; m, meters]

Variables	Mean	Std. dev.	Min	Max
Well nitrate (mg/L)	2.02	3.26	0.00	20.00
Change in well nitrate (mg/L)	0.21	0.70	-2.00	4.10
Area under corn in CZ1 (ha)	0.41	0.97	0.00	9.49
Area under corn in CZ2 (ha)	0.62	1.11	0.00	8.75
Area under corn in CZ3 (ha)	0.76	1.12	0.00	7.89
Area under corn in CZ4 (ha)	0.77	1.06	0.00	6.27
Area under corn in CZ5 (ha)	0.94	1.21	0.00	5.5
Area under corn in CZ6 (ha)	0.87	1.18	0.00	5.95
Area under corn in CZ7 (ha)	0.76	1.00	0.00	5.10
Area under corn in CZ8 (ha)	0.6	0.81	0.00	3.70
Area under corn in CZ9 (ha)	0.62	0.96	0.00	3.86
Area under corn in CZ10 (ha)	0.10	0.23	0.00	0.52
Quaternary thickness (m)	23.61	16.55	7.62	76.20
Well depth (m)	82.78	65.08	20.42	464.80
Leached quantity in CZ1 (kg/ha)	0.26	1.51	0.00	14.91
Leached quantity in CZ2 (kg/ha)	0.00	0.00	0.00	0.00
Leached quantity in CZ3 (kg/ha)	0.53	1.98	0.00	15.85
Leached quantity in CZ4 (kg/ha)	0.58	2.13	0.00	15.95
Leached quantity in CZ5 (kg/ha)	0.66	2.34	0.00	14.72
Leached quantity in CZ6 (kg/ha)	0.55	1.93	0.00	11.93
Leached quantity in CZ7 (kg/ha)	0.34	1.47	0.00	9.89
Leached quantity in CZ8 (kg/ha)	0.01	0.06	0.00	0.35
Leached quantity in CZ9 (kg/ha)	0.00	0.00	0.00	0.00
Leached quantity in CZ10 (kg/ha)	0.00	0.00	0.00	0.00
Fraction of corn area in CZ1	0.11	0.21	0.00	1.00
Fraction of corn area in CZ2	0.17	0.24	0.00	1.00
Fraction of corn area in CZ3	0.20	0.26	0.00	1.00
Fraction of corn area in CZ4	0.19	0.23	0.00	1.00
Fraction of corn area in CZ5	0.22	0.24	0.00	0.94
Fraction of corn area in CZ6	0.22	0.23	0.00	0.90
Fraction of corn area in CZ7	0.25	0.24	0.00	0.85
Fraction of corn area in CZ8	0.30	0.24	0.00	0.86
Fraction of corn area in CZ9	0.30	0.20	0.07	0.73
Fraction of corn area in CZ10	0.09	0.09	0.09	0.09

Table 5. Ordinary-least-square estimates for cumulative nitrate indicator equations.

[Values in parentheses are p-values—***, 99.9-percent level of confidence; **, 97.5-percent level of confidence; *, 95-percent level of confidence. NO_3^-, nitrate]

Variables	Area coefficients	Leached-quantity coefficients
Lag (measured NO_3^- in previous year)	0.93 (0.000)***	0.94 (0.000)***
Capture zone 1	0.07 (0.177)	0.03 (0.44)
Capture zone 2	0.03 (0.67)	0.04 (0.085)*
Capture zone 3	0.002 (0.951)	−0.02 (0.701)
Capture zones 4 to 10	0.01 (0.919)	−0.02 (0.062)*
Quaternary thickness	0.01 (0.381)	0.01 (0.452)
Constant	−0.38	−0.23

Table 6. Arrelano-bond dynamic panel-data estimation results for cumulative nitrate indicator equations

[Values in parentheses are p-values—***, 99.9-percent level of confidence; **, 97.5-percent level of confidence; *, 95-percent level of confidence. NO_3^-, nitrate]

Variables	Area coefficients	Leached-quantity coefficients
Lag (change in measured NO_3^- from previous year)	0.08 (0.736)	0.24 (0.200)
Capture zone 1	2.28 (0.046)**	0.77 (0.000)***
Capture zone 2	5.88 (0.014)**	3.59 (0.000)***
Capture zone 3	1.71 (0.018)**	1.88 (0.000)***
Capture zone 4 to 10	0.10 (0.164)	0.04 (0.000)***
Quaternary thickness	−0.47 (0.007)***	−0.74 (0.000)***

Table 7. Arrelano-Bond dynamic panel-data estimations using three categories of thickness for Quaternary deposits.

[Quaternary thickness: 1, as much as 15.24 meters (m); 2, 15.25–30.48 m; 3,greater than or equal to 30.5 m; area under corn in hectares. Values in parentheses are p-values—***, 99.9-percent level of confidence; **, 97.5-percent level of confidence; *, 95-percent level of confidence. NO_3^-, nitrate; CZ, capture zone]

Variables	Coefficients
Lag (change in measured NO_3^- from previous year)	0.22 (0.438)
Area under corn in CZ1 in Quaternary thickness 1	3.30** (0.019)
Area under corn in CZ2 in Quaternary thickness 1	8.80*** (0.006)
Area under corn in CZ3 in Quaternary thickness 1	2.61*** (0.008)
Area under corn in CZ4 to 10 in Quaternary thickness 1	0.11 (0.194)
Area under corn in CZ1 in Quaternary thickness 2	531.28 (0.89)
Area under corn in CZ2 in Quaternary thickness 2	244.96 (0.89)
Area under corn in CZ3 in Quaternary thickness 2	192.51 (0.89)
Area under corn in CZ4to10 in Quaternary thickness 2	0.90 (0.889)
Area under corn in CZ1 in Quaternary thickness 3	omitted
Area under corn in CZ2 in Quaternary thickness 3	−0.65 (0.943)
Area under corn in CZ3 in Quaternary thickness 3	−7.12 (0.926)
Area under corn in CZ4 to 10 in Quaternary thickness 3	−25.49 (0.921)

For a 40-ha experimental field in southwestern Iowa under annual corn production with regular nitrogen application of 168 kg/ha, Steinheimer and others (1998) found annual nitrogen leaching rates in wells for the period 1969–90 to be in the range of 0.45 to 81.0 (kg/ha) with a mean of 22.76 (kg/ha). For more than 80 percent of the State of Iowa, Libra and others (2004) found that individual watershed outputs range from 3.36 to 38.11 kg/ha. Over the 2001 to 2010 period, our estimates of average nitrate leached (kg/ha) are relatively constant, with the exception of 2001 (table 8). It is important to note that for our results (table 8), the regional, annual averages are compiled from individual HRUs in discrete subbasins, and the range of values for our 2001 to 2010 estimates is 0.0 to 307.6 (kg/ha) with a standard deviation from the mean of 6.76 (kg/ha). This observation would help to explain what would appear to be relatively low estimates of nitrate leaching rates (table 8) in comparison to the literature cited above. Furthermore, the average annual nitrate leaching rate over the entire region could decrease because of the preponderance of low values across the region with the exception of just a few areas with high leachate values (as suggested in the spatial distribution of fig. 19). Finally, the residual nitrogen

left over from previous years' activities is not accounted for in these estimates, as the estimates were produced from simulations conducted on an annual basis. Other studies have focused on nitrate leaching measurements obtained at the outfalls of tile-drainage systems (Weed and Kanwar, 1995; Malone and others, 2010); values from such measurements are not the same as the values in our study, which address the mechanistic model of percolation of water out of the bottom of soil horizons and recharge into the aquifer system, which then relate to nitrate measurements in wells.

The balance of nitrate loading is heavily skewed towards corn production versus soybeans, as would be expected as the result of nitrogen fertilizer being applied to corn crops. The contribution of soybeans to the nitrogen load is a bit more difficult to understand; however, it is a documented phenomenon (Angle, 1990). Possible explanations include the fact that legumes (and their nodules), such as soybeans, are fixers of atmospheric nitrogen and produce ammonia (NH_3) in the soils in which they grow. Consequently, soybeans add nitrogen to the soil, which could already contain a fraction of nitrogen, and the infiltration and percolation of precipitation could mobilize nitrogen down through the soil layers.

Table 8. Average nitrate leaching rates and total leached amount estimated from ArcSWAT for the northeastern Iowa study region, 2001–2010.

[LULC, land use/land cover; kg, kilograms; ha hectares]

YEAR	LULC	Average nitrate leaching (kg/ha)[1]	Total nitrate leached (kg)
2001	Corn	0.60	722,944
	Soybeans	0.27	319,125
Total		0.43	1,042,069
2002	Corn	1.42	2,155,602
	Soybeans	0.34	355,331
Total		0.88	2,510,933
2003	Corn	1.58	2,434,198
	Soybeans	0.31	328,587
Total		0.94	2,762,785
2004	Corn	1.66	2,160,913
	Soybeans	0.34	444,825
Total		1.00	2,605,738
2005	Corn	1.54	2,070,425
	Soybeans	0.33	385,803
Total		0.93	2,456,228
2006	Corn	1.48	2,231,498
	Soybeans	0.31	392,205
Total		0.89	2,623,703
2007	Corn	1.63	2,327,863
	Soybeans	0.30	245,782
Total		0.96	2,573,645
2008	Corn	1.40	2,068,243
	Soybeans	0.33	409,423
Total		0.86	2,477,666
2009	Corn	1.72	2,474,250
	Soybeans	0.30	340,655
Total		1.01	2,814,904
2010	Corn	1.54	2,803,963
	Soybeans	0.28	321,375
Total		0.91	3,125,337
Grand total		0.88	24,993,008

[1]Note: Average nitrate leach rates include hydrologic response units (HRUs) that do not contain any leaching, which drags down the value for the whole year.

Table 9. Proportional hazards model estimated effects of explanatory factors on probablity of well survival (equation 20).

[m, meters]

Variable[1]	Parameter	Estimate[3]	
Depth (m)	β_1	−0.0087	(0.0001)
Time trend (days)[2]	β_2	−0.00022	(0.00002)
Year 1	γ_1	−3.601	(0.056)
Year 2	γ_2	−3.264	(0.035)
Year 3	γ_3	−3.108	(0.018)
Year 4	γ_4	−3.033	(0.013)
Year 5	γ_5	−2.988	(0.010)
Year 6	γ_6	−2.968	(0.007)
Year 7	γ_7	−2.958	(0.005)

[1]Number of subbasin indicator variables=18,615.

[2]Subbasin indicator variables omitted for clarity=603.

[3]Standard error in parenthesis.

Fertilizer nitrate leaching in the study region is mostly in a northwest-southeast trending band (fig. 19). It appears that this band is following the topography and surface drainage pattern in the study region, suggesting that particular riverine systems and watersheds could more susceptible to loading nitrogen into the groundwater system. This spatial distribution is relatively consistent over time, except in 2001 when there was more leachate in the northern subbasins of the study region. It is worth noting that in many HRUs no leaching occurred. This could be related to a variety of factors such as uptake of nitrogen by plants, limited percolation or precipitation, soil characteristics that limited nitrate mobility or caused denitrification, or other factors. Because of the area-weighted average method for portraying the results of our nitrate leaching estimates, the influence of some of the individual HRUs could have been reduced.

Groundwater Vulnerability

In table 9, we provide select variables, parameters, estimates, and standard error results for equation 20 (the probability of well failure; that is that a well doesn't survive as a result of groundwater contamination). For one of the subbasins, table 9 shows that well survivability was observed to be higher for deeper wells, as depth has a negative coefficient and also was improving over time as the time trend and years have negative coefficients, which decrease the probability of well failure. Deep wells are both expected to be inherently less vulnerable to pollution from the surface and also typically valued as important sources for municipal

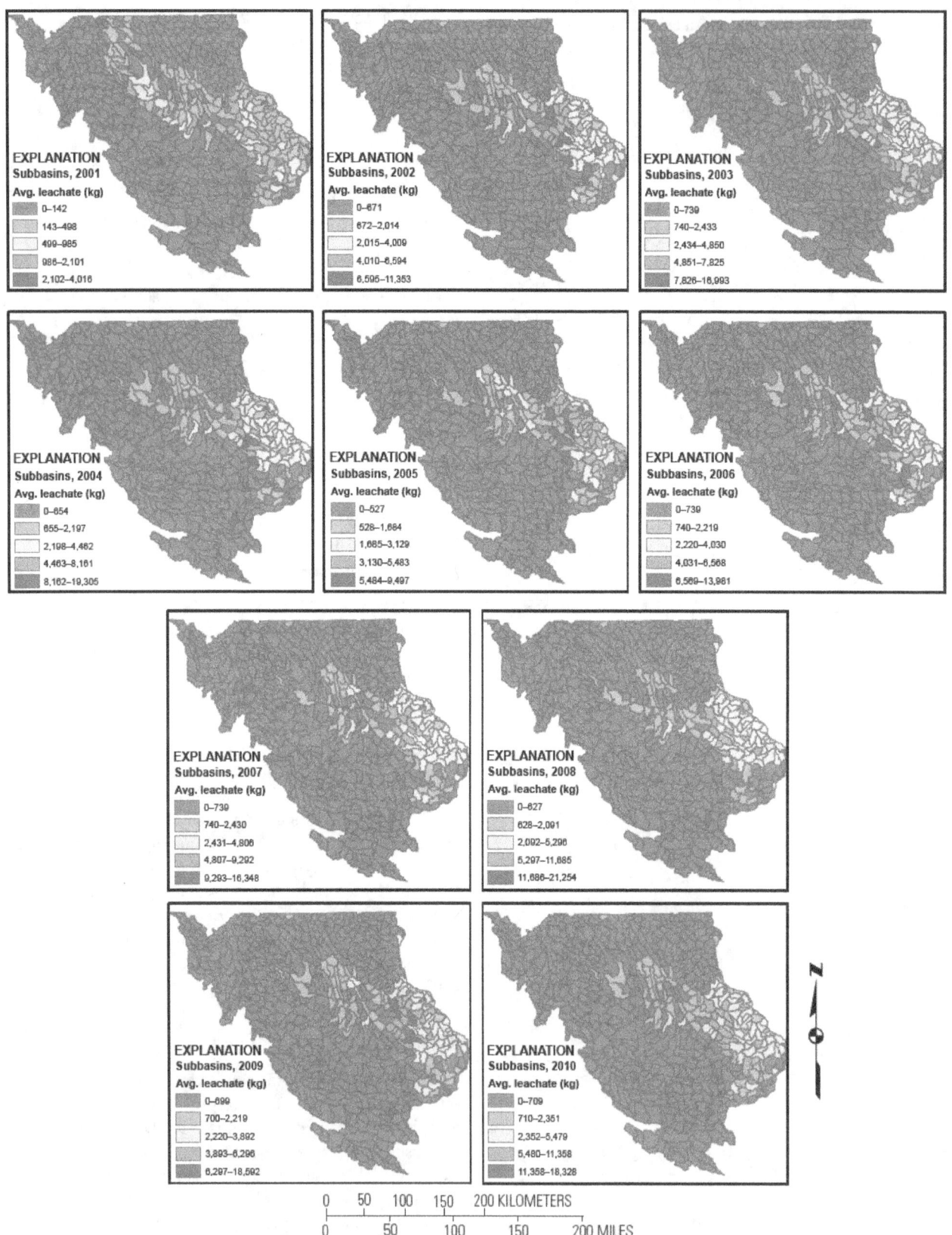

Figure 19. Maps showing subbasin-level nitrate leaching associated with corn and soybean production estimated from ArcSWAT for the northeastern Iowa study region, 2001 to 2010. Avg., average; kg, kilograms.

water supplies, so finding a higher survival rate is reasonable. The survivability of deeper wells is consistent with other studies focused on comparable physiographic areas elsewhere (Nolan and Hitt, 2006; Warner and Arnold, 2010). The increase in well survivability over time is a significant result because—using well survivability as an indicator for groundwater quality—it provides evidence that policies brought to bear in protecting groundwater have been effective. Holding depth constant at 30 m and the date constant at the median date of the data (January 18, 2005), we can plot part of the family of well or groundwater survivability curves for the example of three of the HUC level 12 subbasins in the study region (fig. 20). These curves flatten out after 7 years, so we can effectively summarize the survivability characteristics of a subbasin by the 10-year survival probability (fig. 21). These results quantify the environmental constraint we adhere to in equation 2 when approximating the regulator's problem by maximizing the value of crop production. It is interesting to note that the results from the

nitrate yield and leaching estimates come from different data and models than the groundwater vulnerability estimates, so the higher agricultural production and lower leaching rates for the western part of our study region (figs. 18 and 19) corroborate the higher groundwater survival probabilities (fig. 21) in the same part of the study region.

Value of Information Results

The MRLI VOI is derived from both (1) informing decisions better by applying the statistical population rather than a ground-based sampling approach to estimate the joint output of a regional land-use portfolio (in other words, reducing uncertainty) and (2) constructing an optimal scenario of the landscape using MRLI-derived scientific information (in other words, applying the data) and other geospatial data and models where net crop production can be increased without sacrificing groundwater quality (Wu and Segerson, 1995). The observed value of corn and soybean production in the 35-county northeastern Iowa

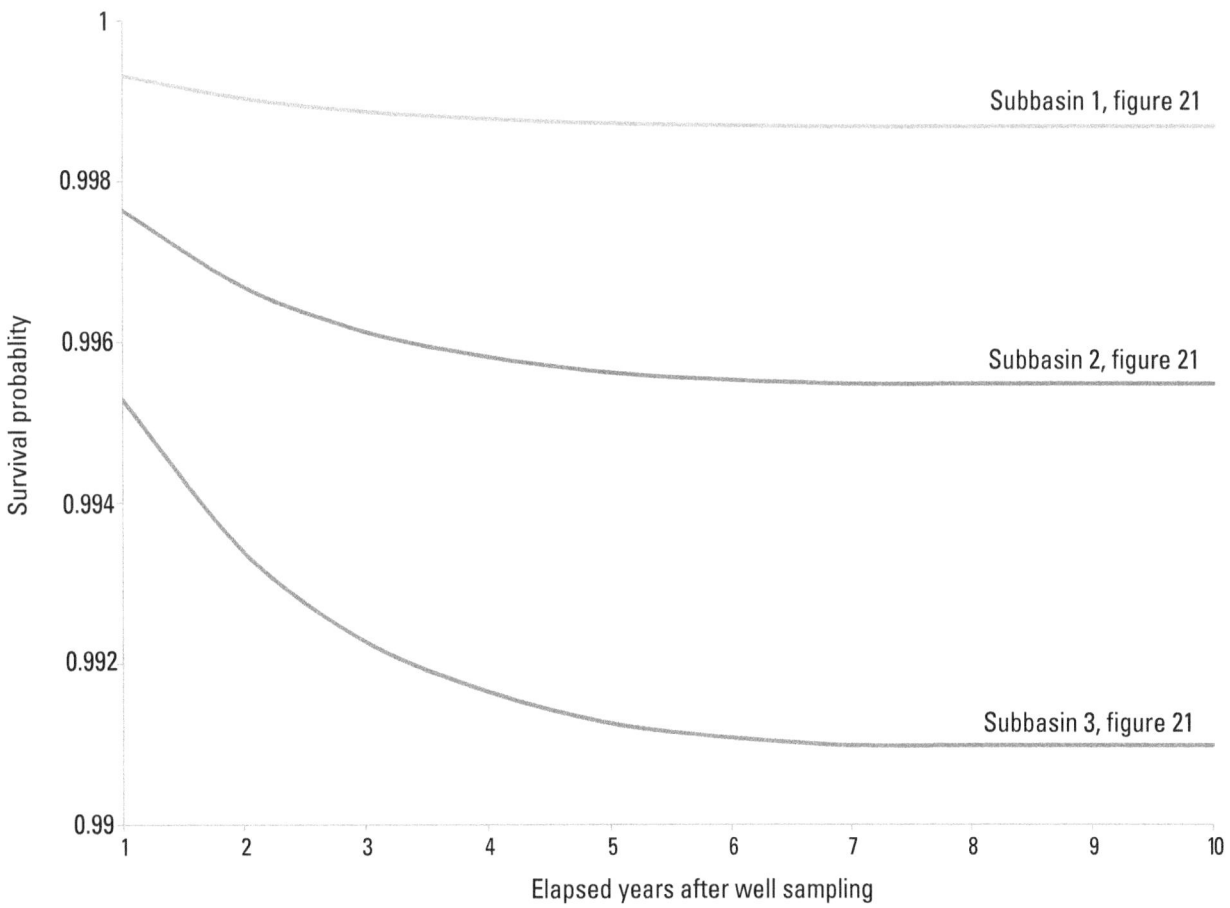

Figure 20. Graph showing groundwater-survival probability curves of three subbasins in the 35-county northeastern Iowa study region. The proportional hazards model was used to quantify the probability that groundwater will "survive" by remaining within the 10 milligrams per liter (mg/L) standard for nitrate contamination. This model was calibrated using data from wells sampled and tested for nitrate concentration by the Iowa Department of Natural Resources and the National Water Quality Assessment Program from wells throughout the study region between 1940 and 2010.

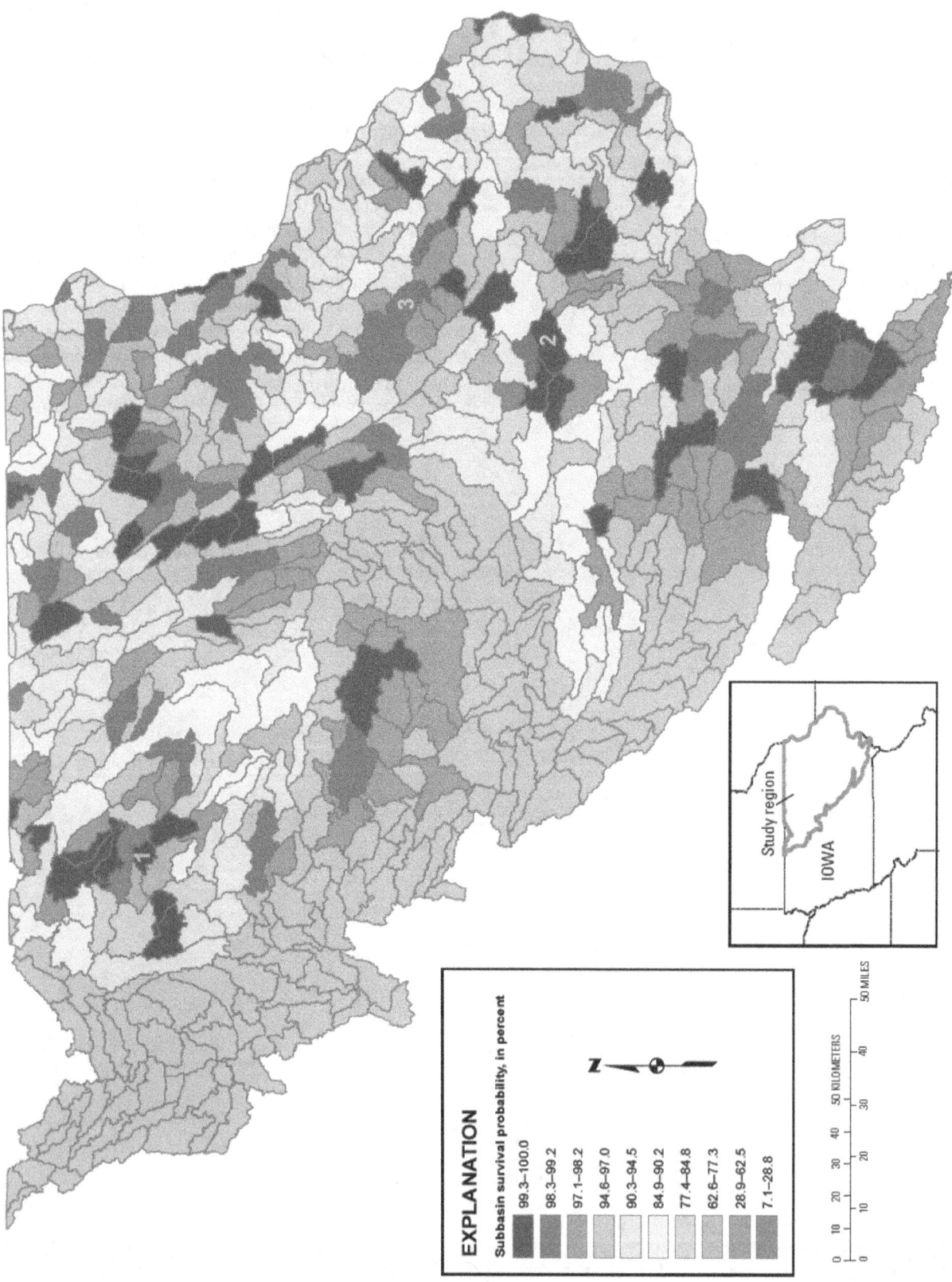

Figure 21. Map showing groundwater failure and subbasin probability of survival for the northeastern Iowa study region. Groundwater-survival probability curves for numbered subbasins (1, 2, and 3) are show in figure 20 and are a result of equation 21.

study region (without MRLI, fig. 22) varied from $2.5 billion to $5.7 billion with year to year productivity variability super-imposed on the increasing real-price trends. By moving corn production to lands identified to be less prone to leach nitrate and additionally to lands with fate and transport properties that render aquifers less vulnerable to leached nitrate, the value of the crop can be increased substantially, while holding level the risk of groundwater contamination. The *EAI* of the increased production during the study period is $858 (±197) million (fig. 22) using the Office of Management and Budget discount rate guideline for public investment of 2.3 percent in Circular A-94 Appendix C (Office of Management and Budget, 2011). This amounts to a *NPV* of $38.1 (±8.8) billion if a similar stream of benefits were to accrue from the MRLI information into the indefinite future. Because the land unit for optimization was at the subbasin level we can map the patterns of increased crop value across the study region (fig. 23).

We have provided the optimal benefit window that policy-makers must work within, and the actual window will certainly

be less than the optimal, but how much less than the maximum benefit will depend on the policy tools considered acceptable and how well these tools are implemented. In concert with the spatially explicit application in this analysis, a number of other economic incentive programs and management policies could be assessed with the IAA to alter the behavior of individuals across the study region. This assessment of potential behavioral change could assess different outcomes for the optimally allo-cated LULC on the landscape. These include:

- Mandated requirements of RFS,

- Farm Bill direct subsidies and changing commodity program payments that would alter relative prices and likely lead to changes and cropping patterns (Wu and Segerson, 1995),

- USDA/NRCS programs that offer long-term conser-vation program contracts that pay to maintain fallow lands in vulnerable areas.

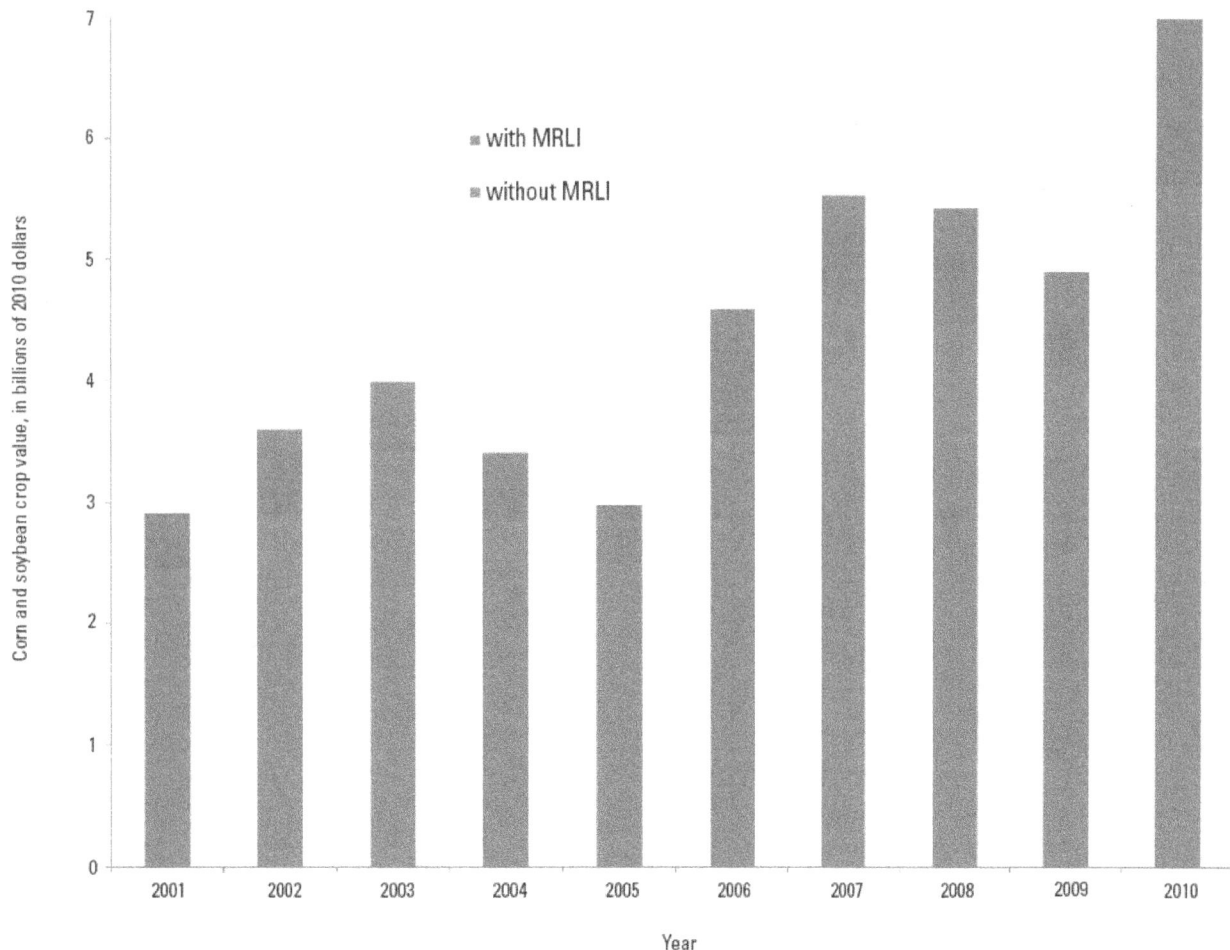

Figure 22. Bar graph showing annual flow of benefits with and without moderate-resolution land imagery (MRLI) for the 35-county northeastern Iowa study region. The value of corn and soybean production using the observed land-use pattern is shown by the blue bars. The higher value illustrated by the red bars would be possible without increasing the risk of groundwater contamination if corn production were moved to lands identified to be less prone to leach nitrate and additionally to lands with fate and transport properties that render aquifers less vulnerable to leached nitrate.

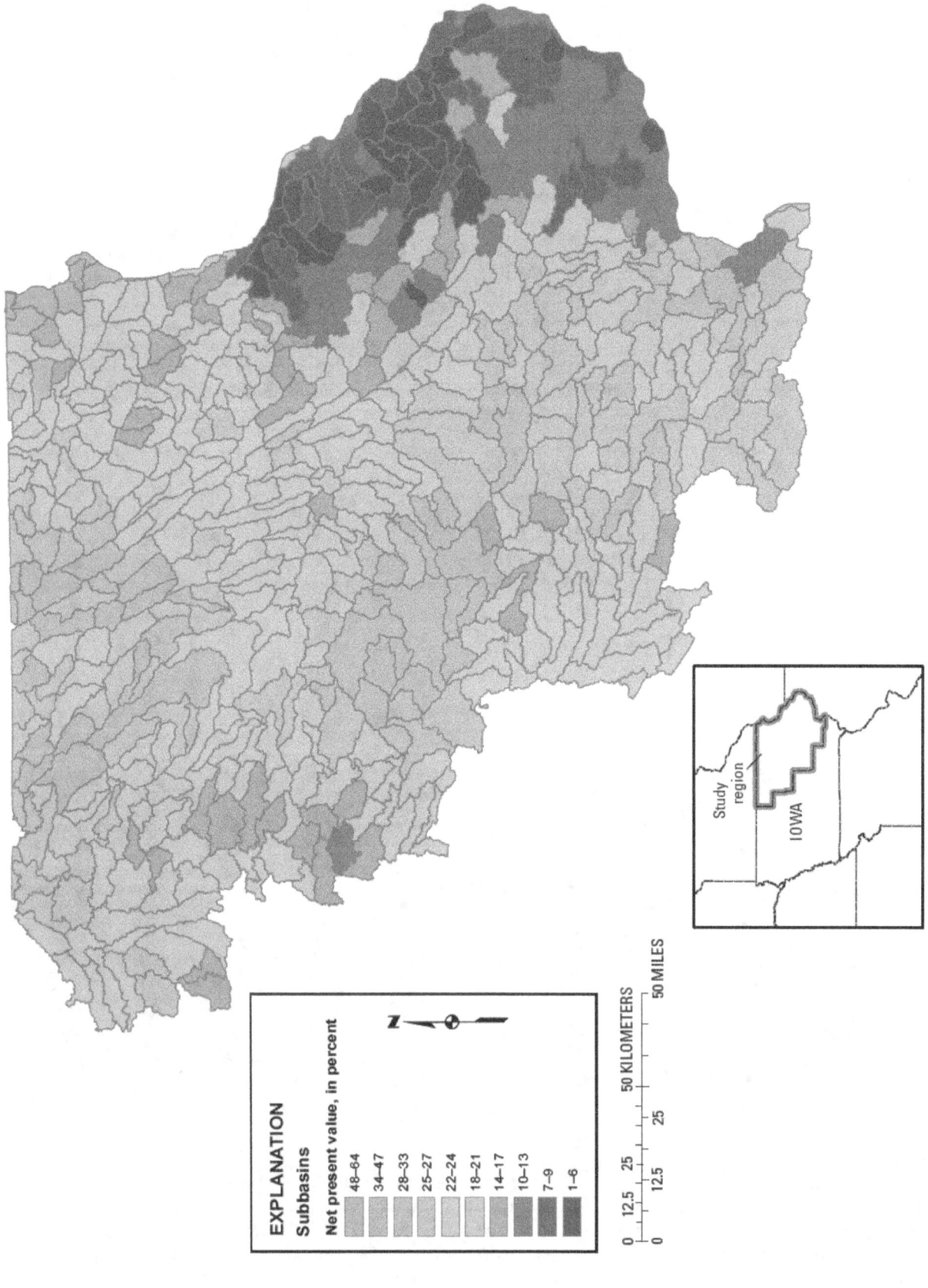

Figure 23. Map showing the net present value estimates for the value of information (VOI) calculations at the subbasin-level that overlap the 35-counties in the northeastern Iowa study region.

- Limit fertilizer application in vulnerable well CZs (Hall, 1992; Fricker, 1983; Andersson and others, 1984),

- Land-use planning in vulnerable areas that includes zoning restrictions for certain land uses, easements on particular lands, and (or) recharge protection zones (Adams and Foster, 1992).

The inclusion of such policies in the analysis would likely decrease the VOI estimates and represent a more realistic allocation of land uses.

Additional Discussion

Using the CDL, and MRLI such as that provided by Landsat as a key input, the agricultural production is well distributed and varied across the time of the analysis and the space of the study region. The reason that the HRUs varied over time was that the LULC classification of the CDL varied over time, as did the source imagery's pixel size. The range in HRUs is important because it provides an indication of the potential heterogeneity of yield, resolution of the analysis (area) and nitrate leachate values, as well as the potential for certain HUCs to have their LULCs reallocated in the optimization routine. It is important to note that although the reporting unit is a HUC or subbasin, finer resolution and spatially explicit HRUs that are not explicitly delineated reflect the site conditions (e of eq. 1) that influence yield (q of eq. 1). It is also important to note that MRLI VOI is inherently related to behaviors observable using the MRLI information, thus because we cannot observe inputs or farm management practices (v and z of eq. 1) directly with MRLI information, we assumed these stayed constant given the crop choice, which we could observe. In future work, a richer model of these practices should be incorporated in a detailed policy analysis to account for predicted changes in unobserved practices that would occur along with the desired changes induced in crop planting patterns.

The spatiotemporal resolution of the yield results are well beyond estimates that are traditionally accomplished with county-level estimates. In comparison to the 35 counties that cover the study region, we provided estimates from 603 subbasins each containing multiple HRUs. The area of the HRUs is generally smaller than 10 km^2 (table 3). The range of county level yields from NASS sampling results in our region in 2002 for corn was 7.62 to 10.97 tons/ha, whereas the range among subbasins from the ArcSWAT calculations in 2002 were 6.40 to 11.55 tons/ha. Because counties aggregate multiple subbasins, the range for counties should be within the range for subbasins, because any county containing an extreme subbasin will also contain subbasins not at that extreme. From 2001–2010, the corn and soybean mean yields (table 3) are comparable to those provided by FAPRI (table 10). On an annual basis, the corn yields from ArcSWAT are both greater and lower than those from FAPRI, and soybean yields from ArcSWAT are generally lower than those from FAPRI, which could be for a variety of reasons related to the parameters, inputs, and management factors of ArcSWAT or how FAPRI collects their estimates. In addition, FAPRI

is reporting national estimates that include a wide range of biophysical characteristics and management practices, whereas our results are provided for just the northeastern part of Iowa. In our study region, estimates suggest that corn crops regularly provide more total yield and mean total yield per HRU than do soybean crops, which is consistent with expectations.

Although this analysis does not include a specific set of policies and (or) economic incentives as presented earlier, the result of such policies is likely to induce changes to land allocation. Agricultural growing areas are more prominent in the northwest of our study region (fig. 18), but our results are highly dependent on the spatial accuracy of the CDL classification as corn and soybeans. Other subbasins in the central and southern parts of our study region are also productive; however, very little production occurs in the northeast of our study region. Available county enrollment in NRCS conservation programs data (National Resources Conservation Service, 2010) was used to determine the past trends of lands unavailable for production (table 11). The highest year of enrollment in the programs was fiscal year 2010, when 2.9 percent of the total lands in the study region were out of production. Overall, the NRCS conservation programs are likely to have little influence on the overall amounts of land in production.

Similar to Bernardo and others (1993b), FAPRI estimates of production can be important to consider for induced land allocation changes. National estimates from 2005 and projections to 2025 of total ethanol production and the feedstock from corn for ethanol production (table 12) suggest increasing production. Furthermore, additional FAPRI national estimates from 2005 and projections to 2025 of soybean production, as well as of soybean oil available for biodiesel production, also suggest increasing production (table 12). If agricultural production in the study region continues to be sensitive to the production of ethanol and biodiesel, the increasing production projected by FAPRI, until a plateau in about 2016 or 2017, is likely to continue to perturb land allocation.

Because corn/soybean production is the dominant use of land in our study region, its value is the dominant component of VOI for the region. If similar results hold for other corn/soybean production regions, then further VOI proportional to the size of the crop is available, because Landsat imagery is collected globally and therefore available for management of any other corn/soybean growing region. Note that a general equilibrium analysis would be necessary for application of this technology in an area large enough to substantially affect the world price for corn or soybeans. The primary general equilibrium result is a shift in the world grain supply curve, so the value of the baseline production is the same, but the unit value of the new production is less than the baseline world price vector.

Future Research

The IAA provides a foundation to pursue a variety of research directions. By varying the MCL, the IAA can be used to assess the survivability of aquifers under a more or less strict nitrate health standard relative to the current standard.

Table 10.   United States corn and soybean production estimates and projections, 2000 to 2026, from Food and Agricultural Policy Research Institue (2012).

[Growing season format number/two-digit year; ha, hectares; t, metric tons]

Growing season	00/01	01/02	02/03	03/04	04/05	05/06	06/07	07/08	08/09	09/10	10/11	11/12	12/13
						Corn							
Area harvested (thousand ha)	29,315	27,829	28,057	28,710	29,797	30,399	28,586	35,013	31,796	32,173	32,941	33,845	34,126
Yield (t/ha)	8.59	8.67	8.12	8.92	10.06	9.29	9.36	9.46	9.66	10.34	9.60	10.06	10.19
Production (thousand t)	251,854	241,377	227,767	256,229	299,876	282,263	267,503	331,177	307,142	332,552	316,168	340,449	347,684
						Soybeans							
Area harvested (thousand ha)	29,303	29,533	29,339	29,331	29,930	28,835	30,191	25,960	30,231	30,919	31,000	30,518	30,009
Yield (t/ha)	2.56	2.66	2.56	2.28	2.84	2.90	2.88	2.81	2.67	2.96	2.92	2.95	2.97
Production (thousand t)	75,057	78,673	75,011	66,784	85,017	83,508	87,002	72,860	80,750	91,419	90,602	89,903	89,183

Growing season	13/14	14/15	15/16	16/17	17/18	18/19	19/20	20/21	21/22	22/23	23/24	24/25	25/26
						Corn							
Area harvested (thousand ha)	35,013	35,375	35,723	35,638	35,759	35,900	35,932	35,843	35,953	36,079	36,128	36,173	36,308
Yield (t/ha)	10.32	10.45	10.59	10.74	10.87	11.00	11.14	11 27	11.40	11.53	11.65	11.78	11.90
Production (thousand t)	361,207	369,712	378,393	382,764	388,867	395,047	400,335	404,023	409,788	415,853	421,014	426,104	432,171
						Soybeans							
Area harvested (thousand ha)	29,880	29,842	29,721	29,868	29,929	29,965	30,010	30,088	30,045	30,012	30,016	30,016	30,285
Yield (t/ha)	3.00	3.02	3.05	3.07	3.10	3.12	3.15	3.17	3.20	3.22	3.24	3.27	3.29
Production (thousand t)	89,521	90,135	90,545	91,833	92,830	93,610	94,484	95,446	96,008	96,638	97,389	98,124	99,742

Table 11. Natural Resources Conservation Service (NRCS) land conservation programs summary for the 35-county northeastern Iowa study region, 2003 to 2011.

[Numbers are tallied from county-level figures in the study region and provided by the NRCS (2010) --, no data/not applicable; ha, hectares]

Program	2003 (ha)	2004 (ha)	2005 (ha)	2006 (ha)	2007 (ha)	2008 (ha)	2009 (ha)	2010 (ha)	2011 (ha)	Cumulative program totals (ha)
Wetland Reserve Program	1,081	1,291	--	851	713	--	499	633	1,386	6,454
Grassland Reserve Program	57	135	335	--	--	--	203	--	--	730
Environmental Quality Improvement Program	--	--	--	25,924	14,867	--	12,202	9,428	13,489	75,909
Wildlife Habitat Improvement Program	--	--	--	323	40	--	295	143	84	884
Conservation Stewardship Program	--	--	--	--	--	--	--	143,932	65,615	209,547
Emergency Watershed Protection Program	--	--	--	--	--	--	--	2,867	4,690	7,557
Emergency Wetland Reserve Program	--	--	--	--	--	--	--	--	10,583	10,583
Annual totals	1,137	1,426	335	27,097	15,619	--	13,198	157,004	95,847	--
Percentage of case study region	0.02	0.03	0.01	0.50	0.29	--	0.24	2.91	1.77	--

More agrochemicals could be added to the model to obtain a comprehensive analysis of the impacts of the chemicals on groundwater. The range of ecosystem services in the model could be expanded to include soil retention and increased productivity, other drinking water quality improvements related to surface hydrology, eutrophication and importance of riparian buffers, habitat preservation and wildlife corridors for biodiversity, wetland conservation/restoration for water purification, and other crops for consumption and biofuels. Analysis of other policy issues is possible, including (1) issues such as tax incentives and user fees to reduce fertilizer use and to reduce the planting of crops with high fertilizer demands (de Haen, 1982; Wu and Segerson, 1995) and (2) economic incentives to adopt best management practices, precision agriculture (a concept that relies on new technologies, such as satellite imagery, to observe and respond to variations within fields), and (or) technological advances in crop strains.

The IAA could be used to assess alternative land management practices. For example, by using a high-resolution, lidar-based bare-earth model, as well as Soil Survey Geographic (SSURGO)[14] soil databases and additional LULC types, certain known hotspots that are susceptible to groundwater pollution could be studied at finer-resolution to focus on management-based scenarios and analysis of nutrient dynamics. Examples include (1) testing the efficacy of shallow-rooted and deep-rooted plants to remove residual nitrogen not taken up by primary crops, (2) analysis of the effectiveness of riparian buffer strips that are widely used across the Midwest to control nutrient loading, (3) using data provided by the IDNR on locations of livestock operations, estimates of their types and numbers animals, and characteristics of their associated waste streams (as suggested by Loeher, 1977; Barth, 1985; Westerman and others, 1985; and Jackson and others, 2000, to address manure as a compounding factor of aquifer contamination), (4) stratifying the landscape into fields, corrals for livestock, liquid manure holding ponds, and manure-treated forage fields for more regulatory relevance to management units and to consider the dynamics of groundwater recharge rates, volatilization, and hillslope gradients on groundwater quality (Harter and others, 2002; van der Schans and others, 2009), and (5) incorporating the hydrologic flow paths and alteration of nitrogen dynamics associated with presence and absence of berms and tile drains.

Modeling the groundwater in our research required certain simplifying assumptions. Future work with the IAA to address groundwater flows and fate and transport of chemical constituents could include improving travel-time calculations and regional representation of the hydrogeologic system with USGS's MODFLOW (modular finite-difference flow model) and ArcSWAT. This could include such simulation and DSS experiments as (1) drilling new wells into locations known to

---

[14]For more information on the NRCS SSURGO database see http://soils. usda.gov/survey/geography/ssurgo/.

Table 12. United States biofuels production and feedstock source estimates and projections, 2005 to 2025, from Food and Agricultural Policy Research Institue (2012).

[L, liters; t, metric tons]

Feedstock source	2005	2006	2007	2008	2009	2010	2011	2012	2013	2014	2015
Ethanol											
Production (million L)	14,780	18,489	24,685	35,237	41,404	49,528	46,818	46,890	50,675	53,907	56,899
Feedstock in ethanol production											
Corn (thousand t)	35,983	45,097	61,710	83,040	101,486	118,844	119,424	112,454	120,786	127,645	133,816
Corn stover (thousand t)	0	0	0	0	5	16	114	408	713	959	1,208
Biodiesel											
Production (million L)	404	970	1,801	2,282	1,817	2,095	3,402	3,666	3,378	3,406	3,454
Feedstock in biodiesel production											
Soybean oil (thousand t)	369	832	1,308	1,333	876	941	1,491	1,413	1,033	1,006	1,019

Feedstock source	2016	2017	2018	2019	2020	2021	2022	2023	2024	2025
Ethanol										
Production (million L)	57,945	58,037	58,169	58,318	58,500	58,675	58,829	58,964	59,084	59,193
Feedstock in ethanol production										
Corn (thousand t)	135,306	134,553	133,882	133,200	132,509	131,802	131,094	130,371	129,644	128,922
Corn stover (thousand t)	1,454	1,723	2,003	2,317	2,691	3,037	3,310	3,536	3,717	3,858
Biodiesel										
Production (million L)	3,500	3,556	3,602	3,637	3,672	3,705	3,736	3,769	3,796	3,824
Feedstock in biodiesel production										
Soybean oil (thousand t)	1,041	1,079	1,108	1,129	1,151	1,169	1,176	1,177	1,159	1,131

have lower degrees of groundwater vulnerability; (2) reducing the amount of pumping and groundwater extraction to increase the mean residence time of groundwater in the subsurface, thereby increasing the chance of such processes as dilution, dispersion, and denitrification; and (3) more explicit inclusion of denitrification processes at depth, the mixture of waters and their ages, recharge compositions, and the spatial variability and heterogeneity of the controlling factors of biophysical processes associated with groundwater (Green and others, 2010). In addition, extending the length of Landsat land-classification archive data included in modeling from 2000 back to 1972 would improve estimation of the survival probabilities of the groundwater.

The IAA can be adapted to conduct analyses at the State level for Iowa, while retaining the spatial explicitness of the geography. Furthermore, the IAA could be used in a greater context to analyze eutrophication of waterways in the Mississippi River watershed and associated hypoxia in the Gulf of Mexico. Nutrient loading from agricultural lands and other nonpoint sources can lead to impacts on commercial and recreational fisheries in the Gulf of Mexico. The control of such nutrient loading in the watershed poses technical and administrative challenges (Dzombak, 2011). The primary technical challenge is addressing the results of nitrogen and phosphorous loads increasing algal biomass in waterways, which when decomposed by bacteria leads to a reduction in dissolved oxygen that then leads to hypoxia and deleterious impacts on aquatic life. The hypoxic zone associated with the Mississippi River watershed is the largest in the western hemisphere

(Brady and Weil, 2002). Because the Clean Water Act's main focus is on point sources and the study of mitigation strategies for nonpoint sources and their implementation, a primary administrative challenge is the lack of regulation and enforcement on nonpoint source control (Dzombak, 2011). Overall, 90 percent of the nitrogen load from the Mississippi River that drains into the Gulf of Mexico has been shown to come from nonpoint sources (National Research Council, 2008). During the period 2000 to 2002, Iowa has been shown to contribute 20 percent of the nitrogen load annually delivered to the Gulf of Mexico by the Mississippi River (Libra and others, 2004). The groundwater orientation of our work and the IAA could be expanded to include surface-water nitrogen, phosphorous, and sediment loading as additional constraints to the economic maximization problem (eg. 2). The regulatory context of the Clean Water Act's primary nonpoint source reduction mechanism, namely the characterization of and opportunities for source reduction through total maximum daily loads, would make this effort compelling. Also, results could be compared to results from the USGS's SPARROW[15] model. The set of decision support tools in the IAA could be formalized to allow for improved modeling and simulation of land-use reallocation, crop rotation, and land management changes that influence nonpoint source runoff and nutrient loading.

---

[15]SPARROW (spatially referenced regressions on watershed attribute) relates in-stream water-quality measurements to spatially referenced characteristics of watersheds, including contaminant sources and factors influencing terrestrial and aquatic transport (http://water.usgs.gov/nawqa/sparrow/).

The IAA could be adapted to larger extents in the Midwest and other locations in the United States. Our study region in Iowa is only a small part of the larger region of the Midwest that produces corn and soybeans (fig. 10). With similar input datasets[16], we could increase the extent of the IAA. Since 2008 at a minimum, the CDL has been produced for the Southeast, New England and the rest of the Eastern States, the Pacific Northwest, and California. Consequently, applying this IAA in those regions would likely increase the VOI for MRLI. The CDL also covers a variety of other agricultural products that have additional value and alternate production practices. These alternate production practices and regulatory frameworks would likely lead to the inclusion of other nonpoint source pollutants and expanded DSSs in the IAA.

Summary and Conclusions

The MRLI provided by Landsat is used widely in several economic sectors in the United States, providing multiple benefits to society (Miller and others, 2011). Quantification of societal benefits from Landsat is of urgent importance in the Landsat Data Continuity Mission (LCDM) and the continued operation of Landsat missions; the next Landsat satellite launch is planned for February 2013. We adapted an IAA to estimate the value of MRLI information in the application nexus of three major sectors, namely environmental science and management application, LULC, and agricultural sectors, which were identified as some of the largest application sectors by Miller and others (2011). The use of the MRLI, other datasets, models, and scientific information provides an improved estimate of the VOI in our study region, because it increased the potential economic value without sacrificing groundwater quality. In the agricultural example we used for the new application of the MRLI archive, the *EAI* of the enhanced landscape configuration is $858 (±197) million, which results in an *NPV* for the remotely sensed data of $38.1 (±8.8) billion (in 2010 dollars) over an indefinite future.

In this research, we developed and applied models for estimating agricultural production, nitrate leaching, and groundwater nitrate dynamics that were coupled with groundwater protection and economic optimization models in an IAA framework to estimate VOI. The models in the IAA incorporated economic, environmental, geological, and hydrological sciences in the land-use management problem and were conducted in northeastern Iowa, which is underlain by Silurian and Devonian aquifers. Also, the IAA is a soft-coupled DSS with the objective of maximizing agricultural production (an ecosystem service) by reallocating LULC, while maintaining the risk of reduced future groundwater quality for potability (another ecosystem service) in an aquifer to a regulated level. The constrained optimization model included two constraints—(1) the risk of exceeding the 10 mg/L MCL for nitrate in groundwater is not increased, and (2) only land used

between 2001 and 2010 for corn or soybean production can be reallocated. The application of the IAA demonstrated how the characterization of agricultural production and its environmental impacts may change with or without the availability of MRLI.

In this analysis, we have demonstrated that MRLI can be used operationally in a regulatory application. Although the example is an abstraction from an actual implementation of an environmental regulation, more constraints can be added to the DSS for regulating the impacts of agriculture on a wider range of ecosystem services. The modeling tools developed here were designed to analyze the ramifications of agricultural production on groundwater vulnerability. The case study demonstrated the VOI of MRLI by providing more accurate agricultural production and nitrate leaching estimates and additional benefits to society by more efficiently allocating production without sacrificing groundwater quality in an agricultural region. Thus, this use of MRLI—in conjunction with other scientific datasets and process models—provides an increase in potential economic value and, hence there is a positive VOI attributed to archived Earth observation data. Our analysis shows that the benefits of the Landsat archive and MRLI could be large over space and time as an operational Earth observation tool for managing land and natural resources.

Acknowledgments

The authors would like to thank the Land Remote Sensing Program for funding and supporting this research, especially Bruce Quirk and Barron Bradford. We would also like to acknowledge the contributions of the USGS WGSC's senior management, namely Mara Tongue, Susan Benjamin, and Larry Gaffney in supporting, reviewing, and overseeing the work. Also, many colleagues and collaborators assisted with the research, laid its groundwork, and provided valuable knowledge, data, and insights without which we would not have been successful in our endeavors. They include Paul Amos (University of Pennsylvania), Larry Beard (USGS), Ron Beck (USGS), Barbara Bekins (USGS), James Calzia (USGS emeritus), Chris Ensminger (IDNR), Mike Gannon (IDNR), Dario Garcia (USGS), Michael Gould (USGS), Christopher Green (USGS), David Halsing (URS Corporation), James Hendley (USGS), Caroline Hermans (City University of New York), Mary Howes (IDNR), Jeanne Jones (USGS), Stephen Kalkhoff (USGS), Leonard Konikow (USGS), Richard Leopold (formerly of IDNR), Lixia Liao (USGS), Robert Libra (IDNR), Molly Macauley (Resources for the Future), Rick Mueller (NASS), Vivian Nguyen (USGS), Alan Rabideu (University of Buffalo), Benjamin Sleeter (USGS), Raghavan Srinivasan (Texas A&M University), Kenneth Steif (University of Pennsylvania), Robert Swanson (USGS), Prasad Thenkabail (USGS), Ate Visser (Lawrence Berkeley National Laboratory), Judy Weathers (USGS), and Tamara Wilson (USGS). Finally, we would like to thank our peer reviewers, Bernard T. Nolan (USGS), Leslie Richardson (USGS), Lynne Koontz (USGS), Holly Miller (USGS), and Benjamin Simon (Department of the Interior) for their thoughtful and insightful comments.

---

[16]The IDNR datasets are available for all of Iowa, as are the rest of the input data (table 1). In other States, if a data gap existed, adequate well data would most likely be the most significant one.

References Cited

Adams, B., and Foster, S.D.D., 1992, Land-surface zoning for groundwater protection: Journal of the Institution of Water and Environmental Management, v. 6, no. 3, p. 312–320.

Amos, P., Steif, K., Wachter, S.M., 2010, Remote sensing classification procedure for identifying corn and soybean crops in Iowa with Landsat imagery: University of Pennsylvania, Spatial Integration Laboratory for Urban Systems, Working Paper no.12, accessed October 2011, at http://gislab.wharton.upenn.edu/silus-research.htm.

Andersson, R., Kindt, T., Johansson, P-O., and Maxe, L., 1984, An attempt to reduce nitrate content in ground water used for municipal water supply by changing agricultural practices: Nordic Hydrology, v. 15, no. 4–5, p. 185–194.

Angle, J.S., 1990, Nitrate leaching losses from soybeans (*Glycine max* L. Merr.): Agricultural, Ecosystems & Environment, v. 31, no. 2, p. 91–97.

Antle, J., and Just, R.J. 1991, Effects of commodity program structure on resource use and the environment, *in* Just R., and Bockstael, N., eds., Commodity and resource policies in agricultural systems: Berlin, Springer-Verlag. p. 97–128.

Antle, J., and McGuckin, T., 1993, Technological innovation, agricultural productivity, and environmental quality, *in* Carlson, G., Zilberman, D., and Miranowski, J., eds., Agricultural and environmental resource economics: New York, Oxford University Press. p.175–220.

Arellano, M., and Bond, S., 1991, Some tests of specification for panel data—Monte Carlo evidence and an application to employment equations: Review of Economic Studies, v. 58, p. 277–297.

Asada, T., 2002, Growth versus environment in dynamic models of capital accumulation: Discrete Dynamics in Nature and Society, v. 7, no. 2, p. 101–109.

Barth, C.L., 1985, Livestock waste characterization—A new approach, *in* Agricultural waste utilization and management: Proceedings of the Fifth International Symposium of Agricultural Wastes, American Society of Agricultural Engineers, p. 286–295.

Bernardo, D.J., Mapp, H. P., Sabbagh, G.J., Geleta, S., Watkins, K. B., Elliott, R. L., and Stone, J.F., 1993a, Economic and environmental impacts of water quality protection policies—Framework for regional analysis: Water Resources Research, v. 29, no. 9, p. 3069–3079.

Bernardo, D.J., Mapp, H. P., Sabbagh, G.J., Geleta, S., Watkins, K. B., Elliott, R. L., and Stone, J.F., 1993b, Economic and environmental impacts of water quality protection policies—Application to the central High Plains: Water Resources Research, v. 29, no. 9, p. 3081–3091.

Bernknopf, R.L., Brookshire, D.S., McKee, M., and Soller, D.R., 1997, Estimating the societal value of geologic map information—A regulatory application: Journal of Environmental Economics and Management, v. 32, p. 204–218.

Bernknopf, R., Forney, W., Raunikar, R., and Mishra, S., 2012, A general framework for estimating the benefits of Moderate Resolution Land Imagery in environmental applications, *in* Macauley, M., and Laxminarayan, R., eds., Value of information—Methodological frontiers and new applications: Washington, D.C., Springer Dordrecht, p. 257–300.

Bock, B.R., and Hergert, G.W., 1991, Fertilizer nitrogen management, *in* Follet, R.F., Keeney, D.R., and Cruse, R.M., eds., Managing nitrogen for groundwater quality and farm profitability: Madison, Wis., Soil Science of America, Inc., p. 139–164.

Bourg, C.W., 1984, Producers' guide to nitrogen management; nitrogen and irrigation management— Hall County water quality special project: Lincoln, Neb., University of Nebraska, Cooperative Extension Service, Lincoln, p. c1–c10.

Brady, N.C., and Weil, R.R., 2002, The nature and properties of soils, 13th ed.: Upper Saddle River, N.J., Prentice Hall, 960 p.

Buckwell, A., 1989, Economic signals, farmers' response and environmental change: Journal of Rural Studies, v. 5, no. 2, p. 149–160.

Bureau of Labor Statistics, 2012, Consumer Price Index all urban consumers (CPI-U)—U.S. city average all items: Bureau of Labor Statistics database, accessed March 16, 2012, at ftp://ftp.bls.gov/pub/special requests/cpi/cpiai.txt.

Canter, L.W., 1997, Nitrates in groundwater: Boca Raton, Fla., CRC Press, 263 p.

Causarano, H.J., Doraiswamy, P.C., McCarty, G. W., Hatfield, J.L., Malik, S., and Stern, A.J., 2008, EPIC modeling of soil organic carbon sequestration in croplands of Iowa: Journal of Environmental Quality, v. 37, p. 1345–1353.

Ceric, A., and Haitjema, H., 2005, On using simple time-of-travel capture zone delineation methods: Ground Water, v. 43, no. 3, p. 408–412.

Committee on Techniques for Assessing Ground Water Vulnerability, 1993, Ground water vulnerability assessment—Predicting contamination potential under conditions of uncertainty: Washington, D.C., National Research Council, National Academy Press, p. 1–11 and p. 42–86.

Delhomme, J.P., 1978. Kriging in the hydrosciences: Advances in Water Resources. v. 1, no. 5, p. 251–266.

Dupuit, J., 1863, Etudes Theorique et Practiques sur le Mouvement des Eaux dans les Canaux Decouverts et a Travers les Terrains Permeables, 2nd ed.: Paris, France, Dunod.

Dzombak, D.A., 2011, Nutrient control in large-scale U.S. watersheds—The Chesapeake Bay and Northern Gulf of Mexico: National Academy of Engineering, The Bridge, p. 13–22.

Eckhardt, D.A.V., and Stackelberg, P.E., 1995, Relation of ground-water quality to land use on Long Island, New York: Ground Water v. 33, p. 1019–1033.

ESRI, 2012, An overview of the map algebra toolset: ESRI Web site, accessed on August 24, 2012, at http://resources.esri.com/help/9.3/arcgisengine/java/gp_toolref/spatial_analyst_toolset_overview/an_overview_of_the_map_algebra_toolset.htm.

Farajalla, N.S., Deyle, R.E., Vieux, B. E., and Canter, L.W., 1993, Correlating nitrate levels in ground water with agricultural land use in Oklahoma, in Proceedings of 1993 Joint CSCE-ASCE National Conference on Environmental Engineering: New York, N.Y., American Society of Civil Engineers, p. 469–476.

Feng, H., and Babcock, B.A., 2008, Impacts of ethanol on planted acreage in market equilibrium: Iowa State University, Center for Agricultural and Rural Development, Working Paper 08-WP 472, 32 p.

Finkelstein, D.M., 1986, A proportional hazards model for interval-censored failure time data: Biometrics, v. 42, no. 4, p. 845–854.

Forchheimer, P., 1886, Ueber die Ergiebigkeit vonBrunnen-Anlagen und Sickerschlitzen. Hannover, Germany, Zeit schrift des Architekted und Ingenieurs Vereins, v. 32, p. 539–564.

Food and Agricultural Policy Research Institute, 2012, FAPRI U.S. and world agricultural outlook: Food and Agricultural Policy Research Institute Web site, accessed January 20, 2012, at http://www.fapri.iastate.edu/outlook/.

Fortin, G., van der Kamp, G., Cherry, J.A., 1991, Hydrogeology and hydrochemistry of an aquifer-aquitard system within glacial deposits, Saskatchewan, Canada: Journal of Hydrology, v. 126, p. 265–292.

Frank, M.D., Beattie, B.R., and Embleton, M.E., 1990, A comparison of alternative crop response models: American Journal of Agricultural Economics, v. 70, p. 597–603.

Fricker, W., 1983, Origins of nitrates in groundwater of the Bunz Valley: Wasser, Energie, Luft, v. 75, no. 3, p. 75–77.

Gheysari, M., Mirlatifi, S.M., Homaee, M., Asadi, M.E., and Hoogenboom, G., 2009, Nitrate leaching in a silage maize field under different irrigation and nitrogen fertilizer rates: Agricultural Water Management, v. 96, p. 946–954.

Greatz, D.A., and Nair, V.D., 1995, Fate of phosphorous in Florida spodisols contaminated with cattle manure: Ecological Engineering, v. 5, p. 163–181.

Green, C.T., Böhlke, J. K., Bekins, B.A., and Phillips, S.P., 2010, Mixing effects on apparent reaction rates and isotope fractionation during denitrification in a heterogeneous aquifer: Water Resources Research, v. 46, W08525, 19 p.

Groffman, P.M., and Tiedje, J.M., 1989, Denitrification in north temperate forest soils—Spatial and temporal patterns at the landscape and seasonal scale: Soil Biology and Biogeochemistry, v. 21, p. 613–620.

Hanson, G.C., Groffman, P.M., and Gold, A.J., 1994, Denitrification in a riparian wetlands receiving high and low groundwater nitrate inputs: Journal of Environmental Quality, v. 23, p. 917–922.

Hall, D.W., 1992, Effects of nutrient management on nitrate levels in ground water near Ephrata, Pennsylvania: Ground Water, v. 30, no. 5, p. 720–730.

Hallberg, G.R., 1989, Pesticide pollution of groundwater in the humid United States: Agriculture, Ecosystems and Environment, v. 26, p. 299-367.

Haitjema, H., 2006, The role of hand calculations in groundwater flow modeling: Ground Water, v. 44, no. 6, p. 786–791.

Harter, T., Davis, H., Mathews, M.C., and Meyer, R.D., 2002, Shallow groundwater quality on dairy farms with irrigated forage crops: Journal of Contaminant Hydrology, v. 55, p. 287–315.

Iowa Corn Growers Association, 2012, Ethanol quick facts: Iowa Corn Growers Association Web site, accessed February 21, 2012, at http://www.iowacorn.org/documents/filelibrary/ethanol/Iowa_Ethanol_talking_points_August__53FE1540A203B.pdf.

Iowa Department of Natural Resources, 2003, Iowa's ground-water basics: Iowa City, Iowa, Iowa Department of Natural Resources, Iowa Geological Survey, Educational Series 6, 92 p.

Iowa State University Extension, 1997, Nitrogen fertilizer recommendations for corn in Iowa: Ames, Iowa, Iowa State University Extension, publication Pm-1714, 4 p. accessed July 19, 2011, at http://www.extension.iastate.edu/publications/pm1714.pdf.

Jankovic, I., 2001, Slit—Win32 computer program for analytic-based modeling of single-layer groundwater flow in heterogeneous aquifers with particle tracking, capture-zone delineation, and parameter estimation, ver. 2.3: 32 p., accessed October 15, 2010, at http://www.orser.psu.edu/GISSupport/SPLIT_Manual.pdf.

Jackson, L.L., Keeney, D.R., and Gilbert, E.M., 2000, Swine manure management plans in north-central Iowa—Nutrient loading and policy implications: Journal of Soil and Water Conservation, v. 55, no. 2, p. 205–212.

Johnson, D.M., 2008, A comparison of coincident Landsat-5 TM and Resourcesat-1 AWiFS imagery for classifying croplands: Photogrammetric Engineering and Remote Sensing, v. 74, no. 11, p. 1413–1423.

Johnson, D.M., and Mueller, R., 2010, The 2009 Cropland Data Layer: Photogrammetric Engineering and Remote Sensing, v. 76, no. 11, p. 1201–1205.

Kapp, J.D., 1986, Implementing best management practices to reduce nitrogen levels in northeast Iowa ground water: Dublin, Ohio, Proceedings of the Conference on Agricultural Impacts on Ground Water, National Water Well Association, p. 412–427.

Keeney, D.R., 1986, Sources of nitrate to ground water: Critical Review of Environmental Control, v. 16, p. 257–304.

Keller, C.K., van der Kamp, G., Cherry, J.A., 1988, Hydrogeology of two Saskatchewan tills, I—Fractions, bulk permeability, and spatial variability of downward flow: Journal of Hydrology, v. 101, p. 97–121.

Keller, C.K., van der Kamp, G., Cherry, J.A., 1991, Hydrogeochemistry of clayey till, 1—Spatial variability: Water Resources Research, v. 27, no. 10, p. 2543–2554.

Kim, C.S., Hostetler, J.E., and Amacher, G., 1993, The regulation of groundwater quality with delayed responses: Water Resources Research, v. 29, p. 1369–1377.

Kolpin, D.W., 1997, Agricultural chemicals in groundwater of the Midwestern United States—Relations to land use: Journal of Environmental Quality, v. 26, p. 1025–1037.

Kross, B.C., 2002, Nitrate toxicity and drinking water standards—A review: The Journal of Preventive Medicine, v. 10, no. 1, p. 3–10.

Kross, B.C., Hallberg, G.R., Bruner, D.R., Libra, R.D., Rex, K.D., Weih, M.B., Vermace, M.E., Burmeister, L.F., Hall, N.H., Cerryholmes, K.L., Johnson, J.K., Selim, M.I., Nations, B.K., Seigley, L.S., Quade, D.J., Dudler, A.G., Sesker, M.A., Lynch, C.F., Nicholson, H.F., Hughes, J.P., 1991, Iowa statewide rural well-water survey data report—Initial analysis: Iowa Department of Natural Resources, Technical Information Series 19, 142 p.

Landsat Science Team, 2008, Free access to Landsat imagery: Science, v. 320, no. 5879, p. 1011

Liao, L., Green, C.T., Bekins, B.A., and Bohlke, J.K., 2012, Factors controlling nitrate fluxes in groundwater in agricultural areas: Water Resources Research, v. 48, 18 p., W00L09, accesed March 16, 2012, at http://www.agu.org/journals/wr/wr1202/2011WR011008/2011WR011008.pdf.

Libra, R.D., Hallberg, G.R., Rowden, R.D., Bettis, E.A., III, Kalkoff, S.J., Baker, D.G., 1992, Environmental geology of Big Spring groundwater basin northeast Iowa: Iowa Department of Natural Resources, Geological Survey Bureau, Guidebook Series 15, 51 p.

Libra, R.D., Wolter, C.F., and Langel, R.J., 2004, Nitrogen and phosphorous budgets for Iowa and Iowa watersheds: Iowa Geological Survey, Technical Information Series 47, accessed July 26, 2011, at http://www.iowadnr.gov/portals/idnr/uploads/water/standards/nbfull.pdf.

Lichtenberg, E., and Shapiro, L.K., 1997, Agriculture and nitrate concentrations in Maryland Community Water System wells: Journal of Environmental Quality, v. 26, p. 145–153.

Loeher, R.C., 1977, Pollution control for agriculture: New York, N.Y., Academic Press, Inc., p. 79–89.

Macauley, M.K., 2005, The value of information: a background paper on measuring the contribution of space-derived earth science data to national resource management: Washington, D.C., Resources for the Future, Discussion Paper 05–26, 30 p.

Malone, R.W., Jaynes, D.B., Ma, L., Nolan, B.T., Meek, D.W., and Karlen, D.L., 2010, Soil-Test N recommendations augmented with PEST-optimized RZWQM simulations: Journal of Environmental Quality, v. 39, p. 1711–1723.

Mas-Colell, A., Whinston, M., Green, J., 1995, Microeconomic theory: Oxford, U.K., Oxford University Press, 981 p.

Matheron, G., 1963, Principles of geostatistics: Economic Geology, v. 58, p. 1246–1266.

Matheron, G., 1967, Kriging, or polynomial interpolation procedures: Canadian Institute of Mining Bulletin, v. 60, no. 665, p. 1041–1045.

McFadden, D., 1975, The revealed preferences of a government bureaucracy—Theory: The Bell Journal of Economics, v. 6, no. 2, p. 401–416.

McKay, L.D., Cherry, J.A., and Gillham, R.W., 1993, Field experiments in a fractured clay till—Solute and colloid transport: Water Resources Research, v. 29, no. 12, p. 3879–3890.

Miller, H.M., Sexton, N.R., Koontz, L., Loomis, J., Koontz, S.R., and Hermans, C., 2011, The users, uses, and value of Landsat and other moderate-resolution satellite imagery in the United States—Executive report: U.S. Geological Survey Open-File Report 2011–1031, 48 p., July 26, 2011, at http://pubs.usgs.gov/of/2011/1031/.

Mirvish, S.S., 1995, Role of N-nitroso compounds (NOC) and N-nitrosation in etiology of gastric, esophageal, nasopharyngeal and bladder cancer and contribution to cancer of known exposures to NOC: Cancer Letters, v. 97, no. 2, p. 271.

Mueller, D.K., Hamilton, P.A., Helsel, D.R., Hitt, K.J., Ruddy, B.C., 1995, Nutrients in ground water and surface water of the United States—An analysis of data through 1992: U.S. Geological Survey Water Resources Investigations Report 95–4031, 74 p. (Also available at http://pubs.er.usgs.gov/publication/wri954031/.)

National Agricultural Statistics Service, 2012, Agricultural prices: National Agricultural Statistics Service Web site, accessed multiple times September 2010 through March 2011 at http://usda mannlib.cornell.edu/MannUsda/viewDocumentInfo.do?documentID=1002.

National Research Council, 2008, Mississippi River water quality and the Clean Water Act—Progress, challenges, and opportunities: Washington, D.C., National Academies Press, 252 p.

National Resources Conservation Service, 2010, Iowa NRCS programs: National Resources Conservation Service Web site, accessed on January 19, 2010, at http://www.ia.nrcs.usda.gov/programs/.

Neitsch, S.L., Arnold, J.G., Kiniry, J.R., and Williams, J.R., 2011, Soil and water assessment tool— Theoretical documentation, version 2009: Texas Water Resources Institute Technical Report 406, accessed January 1, 2012, at http://swatmodel.tamu.edu/documentation/.

Nocedal, J., and Wright, S.J., 2006. Numerical Optimization, 2nd ed.: Berlin, Germany, New York, N.Y., Springer-Verlag, 686 p.

Nolan, B.T., and Hitt, K.J., 2006, Vulnerability of shallow groundwater and drinking-water wells to nitrate in the United States: Environmental Science and Technology, v. 40, no. 24, p. 7834–7840.

Nolan, B.T., Hitt, K.J., and Ruddy, B.C., 2002, Probability of nitrate contamination of recently recharged ground waters in the conterminous United States: Environmental Science and Technology, v. 36, no. 10, p. 2138–2145.

Nolan, B.T., Ruddy, B.C., Hitt, K.J., Helsel, D.R., 1997, Risk of nitrate in groundwaters of the United States—A national perspective: Environmental Science and Technology, v. 31, p. 2229–2236.

Odeh, I., McBratney, A., and Chittleborough, D., 1994, Spatial prediction of soil properties from landform attributes derived from a digital elevation model: Geoderma, v. 63, no. 3–4, p. 197–214.

Odeh, I., McBratney, A., and Chittleborough, D., 1995, Further results on prediction of soil properties from terrain attributes—Heterotopic cokriging and regression-kriging: Geoderma, v. 67, no. 3–4, p. 215–226.

Office of Management and Budget, 2011, Discount rates for cost-effectiveness, lease purchase, and related analyses: Office of Management and Budget, Circular A094 Appendix C, accessed July 23, 2012, at http://www.whitehouse.gov/omb/circulars_a094/a94_appx-c.

Owens, L.B., Edwards, W.M., and Shipitalo, M.J., 1994, Nitrate leaching through lysimeters in a corn-soybean rotation: Soil Science Society of America Journal, v. 59, no. 3, p. 902–907.

Peoples, M.B., Freney, J.R., Mosier, A.R., 1995, Minimizing gaseous losses of nitrogen, in Bacon, P.E., ed., Nitrogen Fertilization in the Environment: New York, N.Y., Marcel Dekker, p. 565–602.

Peterjohn, W.T., and Correll, D.L., 1984, Nutrient dynamics in and agricultural watershed—Observations on the role of a riparian forest: Ecology, v. 65, p. 1466–1475.

Prior, J.C., Boekhoff, J.L., Howes, M.R., Libra, R.D., VanDorpe, P.E., 2003, Iowa's groundwater basics—A geologic guide to the occurrence, use and vulnerability of Iowa's aquifers: Iowa Department of Natural Resources, Iowa

Geological Survey Educational Series 6, 92 p.

Rabideau, A.J., Craig, J.R., Silavisesrith, W., Fredrick, K., Flewelling, D.M., Jankovic, I., Becker, M., W., Bandilla, K., Matott, L.S., 2007, Analytic-element modelling of supraregional groundwater flow—Concepts and tools for automated model configuration: Journal of Hydrologic Engineering, v. 12, no. 1, p. 83–96.

Ross, T.W., 1984, Uncovering regulators' social welfare weights: The RAND Journal of Economics, v. 15, p. 152–155.

Ruddy, B., Lorenz, D., and Mueller, D.K., 2006, County-level estimates of nutrient inputs to the land surface of the conterminous United States, 1982–2001: U.S. Geological Survey Scientific Investigations Report 2006–5012, September 24, 2010, at http://pubs.usgs.gov/sir/2006/5012/.

Rupert, M.G., 1998, Probability of detecting atrazine/desethyl-atrazine and elevated concentrations of nitrate (NO_2+NO_3-N) in ground water in the Idaho part of the Upper Snake River Basin: U.S. Geological Survey Water-Resources Investigations Report 98–4203, 32 p.

Rodvang, S.J., and Simpkins, W.W., 2001, Agricultural contaminants in Quaternary aquitards—A review of occurrence and fate in North America: Hydrogeology Journal, v. 9, p. 44–59.

Schaap, B.D., 1999, Concentrations and possible sources of nitrate in water from the Silurian-Devonian aquifer, Cedar Falls, Iowa: U.S. Geological Survey Water-Resources Investigations Report 99–4106, 19 p., October 28, 2010, at http://pubs.usgs.gov/wri/1999/4106/.

Schlesinger, W.H., 1997, Biogeochemistry—An Analysis of Global Change, 2nd ed.: San Diego, Calif., Academic Press,. 588 p.

Schuh, W.M., Klinkebiel, D.L., Gardner, J.C., and Meyer, R.F., 1997, Tracer and nitrate movement to groundwater in the Northern Great Plains: Journal of Environmental Quality, v. 26, p. 1335–1347.

Silavisesrith, W., and Matott, L.S., 2005, ArcAEM—GIS-based application for analytic element groundwater modeling; documentation and user's guide, draft version 2.13: accessed August 17, 2011, at http://www.groundwater.buffalo.edu/software/ArcAEM/ArcAEM.pdf.

Steinheimer, T.R., Scoggin, K.D., and Kramer, L.A., 1998, Agricultural chemical movement through a field-size watershed in Iowa—Subsurface hydrology and distribution of nitrate in groundwater: Environmental Science and Technology, v. 32, p. 1039–1047.

Strack, O.D.L., and Haitjema, H.M., 1981, Modeling double aquifer flow using a comprehensive potential and distributed singularities 1—Solution for homogeneous permeabilities: Water Resources Research, v. 17, no. 5, p. 1535–1549.

Taraba, J.L., Newton, L., Safley, L.M., Jr., Westerman, P.W., Hill, D.T., Ramsey, D.S., Nordstedt, R.A., and Hegg, R.O., 1985, Research in animal water management in the Southeastern U. S., in Agricultural Waste Utilization and Management: Proceedings of the Fifth International Symposium of Agricultural Wastes, American Society of Agricultural Engineers, p. 257–275.

Tesoriero, A.J., and Voss, F.D., 1997, Predicting the probability of elevated nitrate concentrations in the Puget Sound Basin—Implication for aquifer susceptibility and vulnerability: Ground Water, v. 35, no. 6, p. 1029–1039.

U.S. Environmental Protection Agency, 1994, Nitrogen control: Lancaster, Penn.,Technomic Publishing Company, Inc., , 22 p.

van der Schans, M.L., Harter, T., Leijnse, A., Mathews, M.C., and Meyer, R.D., 2009, Characterizing sources of nitrate leaching from an irrigated dairy farm in Merced County, California: Journal of Contaminant Hydrology, v. 110, p. 9–21.

Varian, H., 1999, Intermediate microeconomics—A modern approach, 5th ed.: New York, N.Y., W.W. Norton & Company, 550 p.

Ward, M.H., deKok, T., Levallois, P., Brender, J., Gulis, G., Nolan, B.T., and VanDerslice, J., 2005, Drinking water nitrate and health- Recent findings and research needs: Environmental Health Perspectives, v. 115, p. 1607–1614.

Warner, K.L., and Arnold, T.L., 2010, Relations that affect the probability and prediction of nitrate concentration in private wells in the glacial aquifer system in the United States: U.S. Geological Survey Scientific Investigations Report 2010–5100, 73 p., available at http://pubs.usgs.gov/sir/2010/5100/.

Webster, R., Oliver, M.A., 2007, Geostatistics for environmental scientists, 2nd ed.: Chichester, U.K., John Wiley & Sons, Ltd., 309 p., doi:10.1002/9780470517277.index.

Weed, D.A.J., and Kanwar, R.S., 1995, Nitrate and water present in and flowing from root-zone soil: Journal of Environmental Quality, v. 25, no. 4, p. 709–719.

Westerman, P.W., Safley L.M., Jr., Barker, J.C., and Chescheir, G.M., 1985, Available nutrients in livestock wastes, in Agricultural Waste Utilization and Management: Proceedings of the Fifth International Symposium of Agricultural Wastes, American Society of Agricultural Engineers, p. 295–308.

Weyer, P.J., Cerhan, J.R., Kross, B.C., Hallberg, G.R., Kantamneni, J., Breuer, G., Jones, M.P., Zheng, W., Lynch, C.F., 2001, Municipal drinking water nitrate level and cancer risks in older women—The Iowa Women's Health Study: Epidemiology, v. 11, no. 3, p. 327–338.

Wu, J., and Segerson, K., 1995, The impacts of policies and land characteristics on potential groundwater pollution in Wisconsin: American Journal of Agricultural Economics, v. 77, no. 4, p. 1033–1047.

Yadav, S.N., 1997, Dynamic optimization of nitrogen use when groundwater contamination is internalized at the standard in the long run: American Journal of Agricultural Economics, v. 79, no. 3 p. 931–945.

Appendixes 1–3

Appendix 1—Integrated Assessment Approach's Assumptions and Their Types

[MRLI, moderate-resolution land imagery; MCL, maximum contamination levels; HUC, hydrologic unit code; HRU, hydrologic response unit]

Assumption type	Assumption
Economic for the producer	Planting decisions are based on current and last season's market prices.
	Profit maximization.
	Decisions are made on an annual basis.
	Marginal changes in production have no impact on market prices.
	The difference between local and national prices is negligible.
	Any modeled difference in sales of grain produced will be sold following the same pattern as the observed sales.
Economic for the region	Partial equilibrium approximation of regulations, R, does not affect crop prices, P.
	Market is competitive and operates efficiently.
	Shifts in the market supply curve are small enough that we can ignore the change in equilibrium price.
	Rational expectations are used, and thus similar flow of benefits from MRLI, value from crops, and MCL thresholds into the indefinite future are expected.
	Risk of groundwater contamination is established by scientific analyses and is a given standard to be implemented for a region.
	Yield for a HUC is estimated as an aerial percentage of a HUC and related to the particular HRUs in the HUC.
	Optimization occurs within a given HUC between HRUs.
Nitrogen loading and leaching	Does not include considerations of population and developed areas that could contribute sources of nitrogen from the use of leach fields, lawns, and sewer outfalls.
	Does not account for atmospheric deposition of nitrogen sources, nor differences in geologic parent materials. In terms of the latter, geologic nitrate is known to persist in organic-rich shales, weather till, and fine-textured lacustrine sediments and is often associated with older groundwater and high chloride and other salts (Rodvang and Simpkins, 2001).
	Does not include many farm management activities that could influence the amount of nitrogen that could enter the hydrogeologic system, such as seed selection, weed and insect management, tillage, tile drainage, reduction of overland flow, and others.
	Assumes the difference in nitrogenous fertilizer application between different corn crops' end use (in other words, grain, silage, food) is negligible.
	Assumes that the agriculture sector is the primary driver of groundwater nitrate pollution.
	Does not consider irrigation as it is minimally employed in this region (less than 1 percent).
	In a given year, leachate is a weighted average of the HRUs in a particular HUC.
Groundwater modeling	Assumes two-dimensional, uniform ambient flow field of groundwater, and not three-dimensional flow.
	ArcAEM and Split computer programs characterize the hydrodynamics at the water table, not at the ground surface.
	ArcAEM and Split computer programs assume no interaction among wells, their site characteristics, and individual operation as may occur in a dense well field network (Ceric and Haitjema, 2005).
	Assumes that the regional approach will not change the net volume (in other words, balance of extraction and recharge) of water in the aquifer systems.
	Does not address post-extraction, technological treatments, such as ion exchange, reverse osmosis, or electrodialysis, as they are remediation techniques for nitrate.

Appendix 2—Nitrogen Cycle

The nitrogen cycle is the cycle in which organic nitrogen is mineralized, plants uptake the mineralized nitrogen, and eventually the nitrogen is returned to the soil in residues. Nitrate is highly mobile in the soil and subsurface. Note that there are a number of other sources and processes at work, where soil organisms are the driving force for reactions in the cycle. The five primary paths of nitrate in the nitrogen cycle are (1) synthesis or immobilization by microorganisms, (2) removal through plant uptake by way of roots, (3) leaching into the groundwater system, (4) volatilization into the atmosphere from the land surface, and (5) re-entry into the atmosphere from the subsurface through denitrification.

Without considering the usage of nitrification inhibitors, soil conditions, timing of application, and other surface and residue management techniques, commercial fertilizers have been shown to lose from ~0 percent to as much as 50 percent of their nitrogen through volatilization of ammonia (Peoples and others, 1995), and—depending on air flow rate, temperature, soil cation exchange capacity, pH and method of application—applied manure can volatilize 21 to 27 percent (Westerman and others, 1985).

Denitrification is often considered the last step of the nitrogen cycle, as it is the major process that returns nitrogen gas (N_2) to the atmosphere (Schlesinger, 1997). The general, four distinct steps of facultative anaerobes completing denitrification are:

$$NO_3^- \rightarrow NO_2^- \rightarrow NO^- \rightarrow N_2O \rightarrow N_2 \qquad (23)$$

Depending on the electron donors, degree of oxygen present, substrates, and other site conditions, more specific characterization of biological denitrification can be described by either heterotrophs that gain energy from carbon oxidation, autotrophs that gain energy from sulfide oxidation, or iron oxidation; all result in the reduction of nitrate (NO_3^-) and the associated byproducts of N_2 and others such as sulfate, iron in two valance states, water, and bicarbonate. In addition to the presence of electron donors, factors known to influence denitrification rates include low topographic positions, shallow water tables and high moisture content, acidity[17], more anaerobic sites, unfractured geologic zones, and clay-rich sediments (Rovang and Simpkins, 2001). Under conditions of snowmelt and rainfall runoff, wetlands have been shown to allow the infiltration of water and transport it laterally outside of the reducing, anoxic environment more often than transporting it vertically to the degree of only 1 percent of precipitation recharged to zones of anoxic till (Keller and others, 1991; Schuh and others, 1997).

Because of solubility and mobility of nitrates in water, once nitrates enter the saturated zone below the water table, the ions are relatively persistent and dispersive. However, if highly anaerobic conditions and an electron donor exist, nitrate concentrations can be reduced by denitrification in groundwater before drinking water is extracted from wells (Canter, 1997). Measuring denitrification is difficult because of its high spatial variability; however, soil texture has been shown to be correlated with denitrification and is considered one of the more reasonable proxies for regional estimates of denitrification (Groffmand and Tiedje, 1989). Considering the importance of landscape position, riparian buffers between agricultural fields and stream courses have been shown to be productive denitrifying zones (Hanson and others, 1994; Peterjohn and Correll, 1984). Although all of these factors and drivers of the nitrogen cycle are not necessarily included in our model, it is important to note their potential influence in our results.

---

[17]Note that high acidity—which can be increased by fertilizers or manures laden with ammonia (NH_3)—will result in reduced denitrification and the production of nitrous oxide (N_2O), which can deleterious influence the atmosphere as a powerful greenhouse gas, a stratosphere ozone depleter, and contribute to the formation of acid rain (Brady and Weil, 2002; Schlesinger, 1997).

Appendix 3—Kriging of Hydraulic Conductivity

Kriging is a geospatial technique for interpolating values for a variable in an unobserved location using neighboring point observations (Webster and Oliver, 2007). The kriging method was developed by Matheron (1963, 1967). This method was introduced to study complex hydroscience systems by Delhomme (1978). Regression kriging (RK) was introduced by Odeh and others (1994, 1995). In addition to the spatial autocorrelation used in the ordinary kriging method, RK includes both the environmental autocorrelation and spatial autocorrelation to interpolate variables for unobserved locations. The RK involves kriging the variable using a regression estimator with environmental (hydrogeological) variables that have a neighborhood trend. The prediction uncertainties are then included by incorporating the regression errors into the kriged variables.

Hydraulic conductivity (HC) depends on hydrogeological properties of an aquifer[18], suggesting environmental and spatial autocorrelation could matter. Therefore, an attempt was made to krige HC surfaces using regression kriging. The HC was regressed using combinations of transformed variables and the best estimation of a log-log regression equation for reducing wide ranging quantities to smaller ranges. For the RK technique, the regression equation for the all aquifers in the study region is:

$$\ln HC = \beta_1 + \beta_2 \ln EB + \beta_3 \ln Th + \beta_4 \ln AQ + \varepsilon \quad , \tag{24}$$

where β is the estimate of the coefficient, EB is the base elevation of the aquifer, Th is the thickness of the aquifer, AQ the type of aquifer, and ε is the regression remainder. Table 13 provides the variables and their parameter estimates. The HC regression layer was created using the ArcGIS spatial analyst tool (fig. 24). The residuals are kriged (fig. 25) and added to the regression-estimation-kriged layer to obtain the final kriged layer (fig. 26) for the variable HC. Thus, a spatially interpolated HC surface was used to derive HC values for the wells without HC information for the purposes of delineating capture zones (CZs) for a larger number of wells.

Table 13. Log-log regression equation for kriging of hydraulic conductivity in Devonian and Silurian aquifers in the northeastern Iowa study region.

Variables	Estimated parameters[1]
Base elevation	1.93 (0.12)***
Thickness	−0.317 (0.06)***
Aquifer type (dummy)	1.92
Constant	−9.74
R^2	0.8088

[1]Numbers in parentheses are standard errors—***, significant at 99.5-percent confidence level.

---

[18] During the course of the analysis, it was noted that geologic faults bisected the Silurian aquifer. Their presence influenced the approach and results of ordinary kriging techniques.

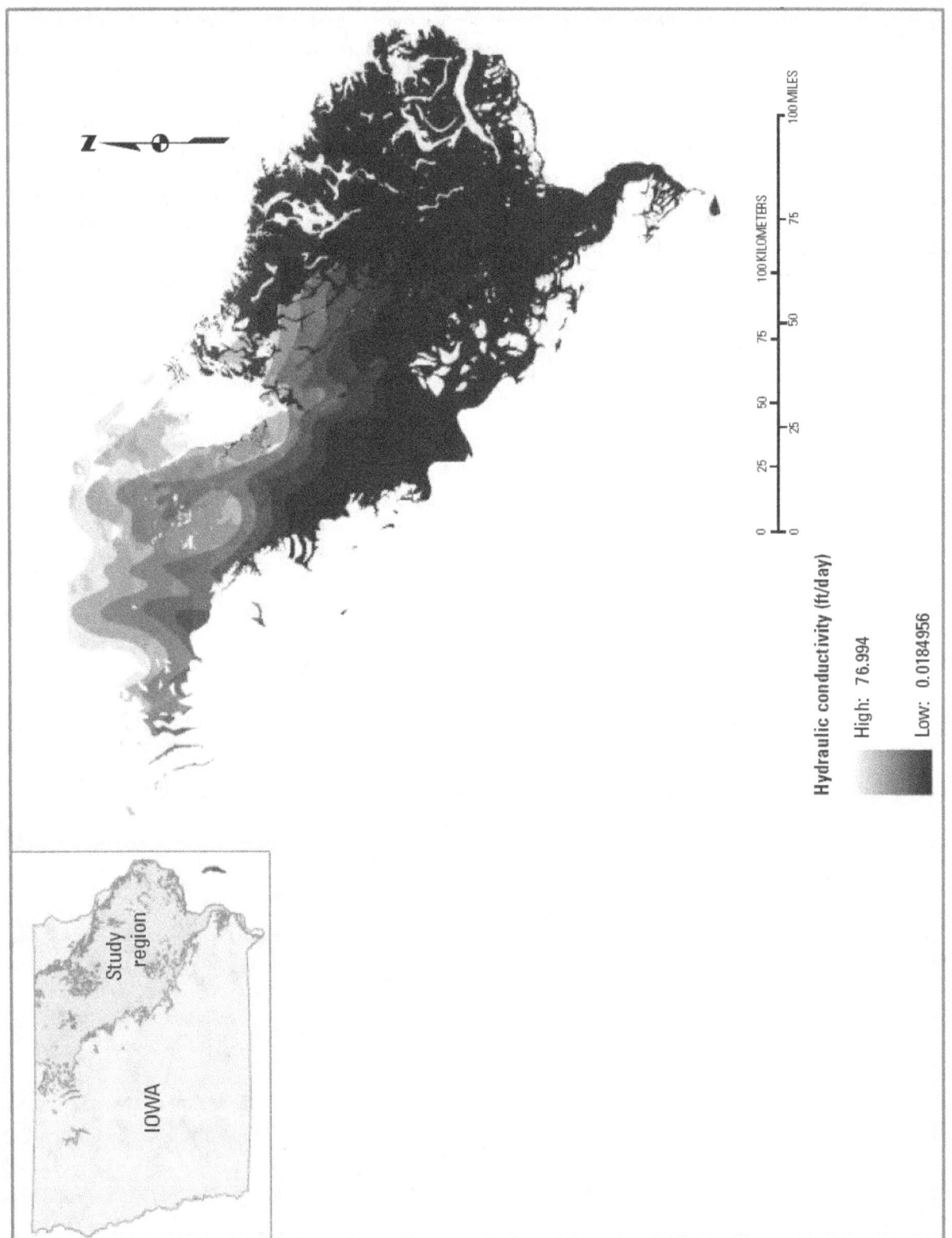

Figure 24. Image of regression kriging without residuals, using hydraulic conductivity for the 35-county northeastern Iowa study region as an example. ft/day, feet per day.

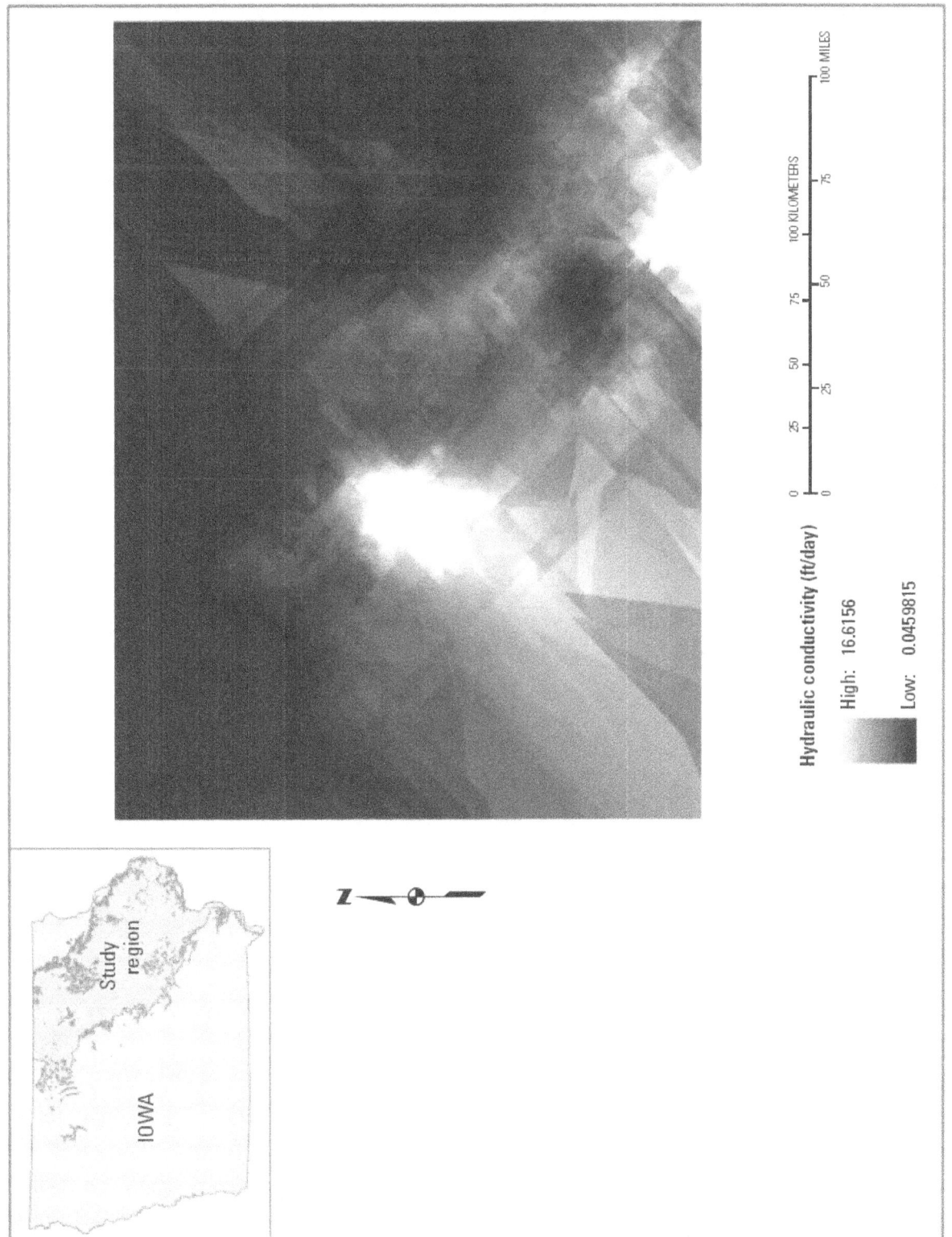

Figure 25. Image of final regression kriged layer, using hydraulic conductivity for the 35-county northeastern Iowa study region as an example. ft/day, feet per day.

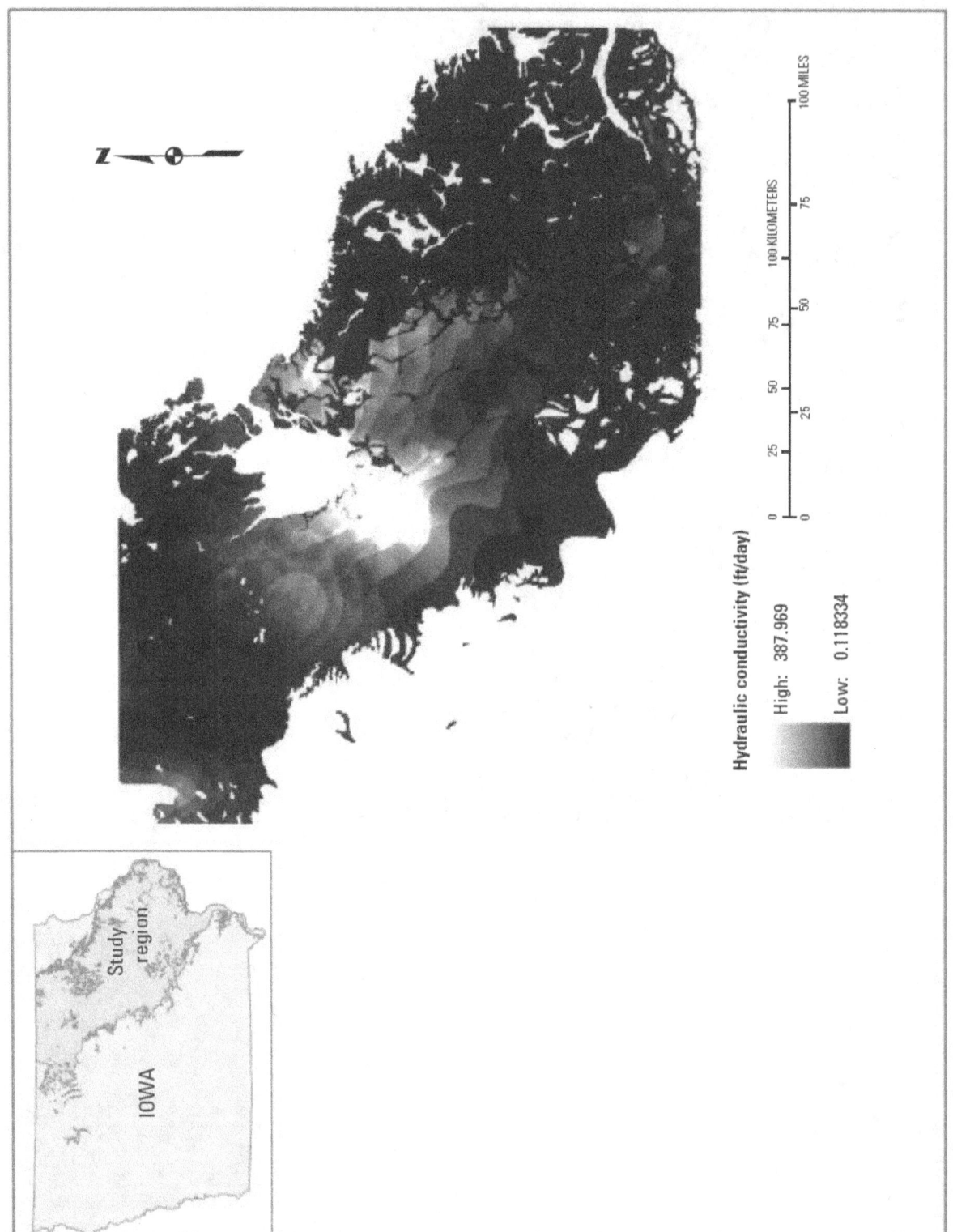

Figure 26. Image of final regression kriged layer, using hydraulic conductivity for the 35-county northeastern Iowa study region as an example. ft/day, feet per day.